JESUS' CALL
TO HIS HARVEST FIELD
Adventures in the Mission Field

Behold, I say to you, lift up your eyes and look at the fields, for they are already white for harvest! (John 4:35)

Ask the Lord of the harvest, therefore, to send out workers into his harvest field. (Matthew 9:38 NIV)

By: Vicki and David Creel

Jesus' Call to His Harvest Field – Adventures in the Mission Field
Copyright © 2021 Maria Victoria P. Creel and David Lucian Creel
thecreels.org

All rights reserved. No portion of this book may be reproduced, stored in a retrieval system, or transmitted in any form or by any means-electronic, mechanical, photocopy, recording, scanning or other-except for brief quotations in critical review or articles, without prior written permission of the publisher.

Unless otherwise noted, Scriptures taken from the New King James Version©. Copyright © 1982 by Thomas Nelson, Inc. Used by permission. All rights reserved.

Other Scripture quotations taken from The Holy Bible, *New International Version®*, *NIV®*. Copyright © 1973, 1978, 1984, 2011 by Biblica, Inc.® Used by permission. All rights reserved worldwide.

Cover Image by: iStock

ISBN 978-0-578-97439-2 (paperback)
ISBN 978-0-578-97440-8 (eBook)

Library of Congress Control Number: TXu002283658

Printed in the United States of America

FOREWORD

When Vicki came to study at SIFAT, we recognized immediately that she was an unusually talented and mature Christian. We did not know the details of how God had led her through many trials to help her develop spiritually until she wrote her story in this book. I have been blessed beyond what any words can express by having the opportunity to read this manuscript where she gives witness to incredible situations that she could not overcome alone. But God could, and He enabled Vicki to grow strong spiritually as she trusted Him while serving in mission for ten years in China, and other tenures in Bolivia and Alabama. This book will inspire those who read it to catch a greater vision of the Power and Love of God and how He is ready to lead us all into greater fields of service for Him.

Vicki gives encouragement to those trying to serve in cross-cultural situations. We can learn so much from her writing how to reach people for Christ in other socio-economic groups in our own neighborhood as well as in different cultures in other countries as she recounts how she dealt with strange food and dark, rainy, freezing days with little heat in her tiny apartment. She learned to go out among the poor where the people had no bathrooms. Once she had to go seven days without a shower and a toilet.

Daily she faced the frustration of communicating in a very hard-to-learn language. When she began to understand and be able to talk in the language, she was hindered from answering people who asked her about God when officials were there to report any foreigner who spoke about God. And foreigners had to live in the cities and only occasionally had the opportunity to travel to get acquainted with the rural people. Vicki faced sickness and loneliness because until she learned the language there were only two other missionaries also learning the language to whom she could talk. The three had no church to go to so they made their own. They were thrilled when a few Chinese Christians joined them.

Through it all, she learned to depend on God. She reminds us of I Samuel 24:24 where David says, *I will not make an offering to the Eternal One, my True God, that has cost me nothing.* She has been willing to pay the price, whatever it cost her in stress, loneliness, or hardship, because to serve Jesus is worth everything it could cost, even if it be our lives. This book is a thrilling witness to that fact.

Vicki tells how she learned that God meets us in different and sometimes surprising ways to connect with us on our level. She learned that relationships with people prepared them to want to know Christ also. So, she and her missionary partners often invited neighbors to eat with them on the holidays, especially Easter and Christmas. They could explain the holiday dishes we eat in our culture and then share why we celebrate these holidays. A number of times people made decisions to follow Christ at these meals the missionaries served them. She also says listening to their own concerns and sharing their grief was a way of building relationships which could lead to their understanding of who God is for them too. Once while sharing with a group in a hotel room, a local friend wanted to give her life to Christ and wanted to be baptized, so they baptized her in the bathtub. She also emphasized that it was important to work with the local churches and get new converts plugged into a Christian fellowship to help them after she had to leave.

There are government-approved churches in China, over which the government holds strict control. Many Christians meet in house churches where they have freedom to worship and talk of the scriptures as they feel led. Often these Christians are in danger of police taking them to jail as the government frowns on these house churches. One Christian told Vicki going to jail was almost as common as eating a meal to them. At first, they would pay a heavy fine to get out of jail, and then they realized that the jailer was just extorting money from them. They decided not to pay it and remain in jail as they found that the jails were a mission field for them. Many who were jailed for their faith led other prisoners to Christ. They taught Vicki that God could use any circumstance for His glory if they would just be open to accept what happened and let God work through them. Vicki explains many of the struggles the members of the house churches face daily.

One of their problems is their pastors cannot go to a Bible School or Seminary and not all of the members have Bibles to read themselves. So, when cultic groups twist the Bible and try to pull the house groups into their cult, they cannot always discern what is true because the members, nor the pastors have had a chance to study the Bible as they want to.

This book is a witness for how our God can take any situation and bring good out of it. Reading it can lift a person from depression to praise, from a hum-drum life to one of walking with God daily, from disillusionment with uncomfortable circumstances to rejoicing because God is in control, and He promises in Romans 8:28 to bring good out of all things for those who love Him. Even when Vicki lost her passport – which could have resulted in getting her thrown out of the country – the great stress, time and financial cost that was needed to get a new one led to one of the greatest experiences she had while in China. Read the book and find out many wonderful true stories that this special Servant of God has gone through as she faithfully served Him in Asia, South America, and North America.

Today Vicki is married to David Creel, a missionary radio engineer, and they serve together keeping Christian radio stations on the air in many countries across our world. Her years of serving as a missionary in China, Bolivia, and Alabama have prepared her to go into all the world together with David, to preach the Gospel of our Lord Jesus Christ.

Sarah Corson
Co-founder of Servants in Faith and
Technology (SIFAT)
Author of *Risking Everything*

TABLE OF CONTENTS

FOREWORD	2
ACKNOWLEDGMENTS	8
DEDICATION	9
IN LOVING MEMORY	10
INTRODUCTION	12
PART 1 – VICKI CALLED TO THE HARVEST FIELD	14
1. A Humble Beginning	18
2. Trying to Run Away like Jonah	31
3. A Fresh Start	35
4. The First Trip	42
5. More Preparation and Mission Training	56
6. The Waiting	64
7. A New Chapter Begins	70
8. Food, Cooking, and Culture	91
9. Seeds Planted and Lessons Learned	101
PART 2 – VICKI IN THE HARVEST FIELD	107
10. Stories of Faith and Faithfulness	109

11. The Paper-cut Man	118
12. Sweet Fellowship with Jesus	125
13. Heroes of Faith and Their Challenges	132
14. Visit to a Village	145
15. The Young People	157
16. Friends in the Mountain City	172
17. Christmas Time	193
18. Special Friends	210
PART 3 – DAVID CALLED TO THE HARVEST FIELD	225
19. David's Story	226
20. Called Together to the Harvest Field	237
AFTERWORD	245
SPECIAL THANKS	249
ABOUT THE AUTHORS	250
NOTES	251

ACKNOWLEDGEMENTS

I want to thank our Lord for His wisdom and guidance as I navigated the uncharted waters of writing and publishing my first book. I am grateful for those who helped David and me write and publish our story, to *"...make known His deeds among the peoples!"* (*Psalm 105:1*)

Thanks to the late Dr. Marcia Anderson and Ms. Li Juaneza, for their friendship and labor of love in editing this book. I also want to thank friends and family for their encouragement and contributions in writing some parts of the story, especially to Mary Kelly, my sister Fey, and Ms. Sarah Corson. Thank you, Randall Murphree (American Family Association), Anne McNabb, and Laura Salmon for your labor of love in proofreading. Thank you, Gary Ragsdale, for your help with the cover design.

I also thank my loving husband David Creel for his love, support, and encouragement. To our ministry partners in Jesus' harvest field, thank you all for your prayers and support. To everyone who prayed with us and helped with research and support to print this book, thank you very much! You all are part of this story, His story.

To my Lord Jesus Christ, I give all the praise and glory!

DEDICATION

This book is dedicated to my Lord Jesus Christ, my Creator, and the Author of my life. I also want to dedicate this book to all who have prayed and supported me in the past with my mission work: churches, individuals, friends, and mission organizations. Your prayers and financial support have kept me on the mission field. The Lord knows your names. *"For God is not unjust to forget your work and labor of love which you have shown toward His name, in that you have ministered to the saints, and do minister."* (Hebrews 6:10)

I also want to dedicate this book to all those who are doing the work of the Great Commission – whether in prayer, financial support or as a 'goer' (missionary in the field). To those who will answer the call of our Lord Jesus Christ to the harvest field, this book is for you!

In Loving Memory of Dr. Marcia Anderson

Dr. Marcia Anderson (Ma'am Marcia) was a retired missionary with the Church of God, Cleveland Tennessee. She held a Doctor of Theology degree from the South East Asia Graduate School of Theology in Manila, Philippines. She taught Old Testament classes and Hebrew at Asian Seminary of Christian Ministry (ASCM) in Manila from 1996-2006. She also became the Dean of Students. She moved to Africa in 2006 and became a professor at Discipleship College, Eldoret, Kenya.

Ma'am Marcia came to ASCM just after I left the seminary to prepare for my mission work in China. I met her during a visit to ASCM during one of my furloughs. We became good friends. I enjoyed visits with her during every furlough. We enjoyed sharing stories and ministry updates over meals she prepared. I appreciated her support of my ministry, too. When she moved to Africa, and I moved to other places, we lost communication. When I got married and moved to the USA in 2014, after some years, our paths crossed again. I was excited to see her when she came to North Alabama to visit a friend in 2015. She told me of her adventures in Africa while teaching at the Bible College. During that time, I began working on this book again, and she kindly offered to help with editing and guidance in writing this story. She also gave me courage to finish writing this book. I thank our Lord Jesus for her inspiration and dedication in serving Him in the mission field. I'm grateful and blessed to have had Dr. Marcia Anderson as a teacher, mentor, and friend.

Dr. Anderson wrote and published several books including The Shepherd's Network and The Finger of God in the Muslim World.

On April 29, 2021, she finished the race and received the crown of life (2 Timothy 4:7-8). She has completed her part in *following Jesus' call to His harvest field*.

INTRODUCTION

    Since I said "Yes!" to *Jesus' call to His harvest field*, my life has never been the same. He brought me to places I never dreamed I could go and enabled me to do things I never thought I could do. However, it was not always an easy journey. Jesus was faithful and true when He said to His followers, *"Go therefore and make disciples of all the nations…and lo, I am with you always, even to the end of the age." (Matthew 28:19-20)*. The best part of the journey in pursuing His call is getting to know Him in every situation and place into which He brings me. Besides the changes He has done in my life, I have had the privilege to see how the Gospel and the love of God have changed other lives too.

    I am grateful and humbled that God still uses me despite my weaknesses, shortcomings, and failures. Some of the names in the stories are changed for security reasons, but they are real people telling real experiences that happened in real places. I have also included realities of living in a cross-cultural setting which God used to "smooth out" some rough edges in me. The Lord also taught me some life and faith lessons through the different experiences and people I met along the way.

    My prayer is for many to be inspired through this story – a story of God's love, faithfulness, and goodness. It is my hope also for some to glean and learn good lessons from my past experiences and failures. My earnest prayer is that many will be inspired to answer **Jesus' call to His harvest field** –

to have a passion for Him and compassion for the lost. According to some missiologists, over 3 Billion people are still waiting to hear the Gospel. So, hear His voice, and receive His invitation, *"Do you not say, 'There are still four months and then comes the harvest'? Behold, I say to you, lift up your eyes and look at the fields, for they are already white for harvest!" (John 4:35)*

"But you shall receive power when the Holy Spirit has come upon you, and you shall be witnesses to Me in Jerusalem, and in all Judea and Samaria, and to the end of the earth." (Acts 1:8)

"For God so loved the world that He gave His only begotten Son, that whoever believes in Him should not perish but have everlasting life." (John 3:16)

PART 1

VICKI CALLED TO THE HARVEST FIELD

"For you see your calling, brethren, that not many wise according to the flesh, not many mighty, not many noble, are called. But God has chosen the foolish things of the world to put to shame the wise, and God has chosen the weak things of the world to put to shame the things which are mighty; and the base things of the world and the things which are despised God has chosen, and the things which are not, to bring to nothing the things that are, that no flesh should glory in His presence." (1 Corinthians 1:26-29)

The Call

I thought my life seemed perfect. I had a good job. I was involved in church ministry. I was only twenty-three! Still there was a restlessness in my spirit. I felt there was something more. It was not like a feeling of "the grass is greener on the other side of the fence." It was a different kind of feeling. Something in my spirit was stirring and I was not sure what it was. Life was busy with a full-time accounting job in a successful corporation, while most of my free time, evenings, and weekends, were busy with church activities, too. Thankfully, I managed to have a few minutes of quiet time in the early mornings for Bible reading and prayer. I thought I had a full life and a good future ahead of me. However, I felt God was trying to tell me something, but I needed time to sit and listen.

Then I remembered a retreat place our church had visited a while back. The place is called, "Prayer Mountain." It was a place on the eastern part of Luzon just outside Metro Manila. It was a nice retreat center built by a church group especially for Christians who want to focus on prayer.

I usually worked Saturday mornings but on one weekend in June 1992, I took some time off and went to the Prayer Mountain to spend a special time with God. With city traffic, it took me about three hours of public transportation to arrive at the retreat facility, nestled on top of a mountain range, away from the busy city. Besides the main sanctuary for church services, the place had big rooms to accommodate a hundred people who came to stay for a few days. There were special rooms also for people who stayed for an extended time and for those who came for prayer and fasting. There were also tiny rooms like cubbyholes just for prayer.

A staff worker gave me a key to one of the cubbyholes. Each floor of the building had about twenty cubbyholes. Each room was about 3x5 feet, had a small table to hold a Bible, a small foam pad to kneel on, a wall fan, and a small light bulb. The small prayer room provided me a space to be quiet and have focused time with God. I stayed there almost all day; I sang worship songs, read my Bible, and prayed. I felt the tangible presence of God. The Word of the Lord in James 4:8 became real to me: *"Draw near to God and He will draw near to you."* Jeremiah 29:13 says, "You will seek Me and find Me, when you search for Me with all your heart."

"Lord what is it that You want me to do?" I asked. Then I felt in my spirit that He said something like, "I am calling you to a great mission." (It came like writing on the wall, in English). I said, "Mission? What do you mean? Are you calling me to mission work?" I asked for further confirmation through His word. "Please give me a verse if you are calling me." He gave me Matthew 9:37-39. At that time, I had not yet memorized the Scriptures. So, I opened the Bible and read, **"The harvest truly is plentiful, but the laborers are few."** Then I asked Him again. "How do I do that? Where do I start?" Many questions floated through my mind.

At that time, the only Christian group I knew was my local church and its mother organization. I did not know any mission agencies, nor had I ever met a missionary. Although I had read some stories of missionaries, I did not even know how to find a mission agency. Through some books I read, I heard about African Inland Mission and Open Doors; I thought maybe I could write to them. The books I had read, though, were mostly very old. What if those addresses were too old and were not valid anymore?

Some of the stories I read from the lives of missionaries like Corrie Ten Boom, Brother Andrew of Open Doors, and others, quickened my interest in missions. There was also a story of a married couple who had gone to Africa for missions. The stories of their life in the bush with the lions and tigers walking around their hut fascinated me. I started to dream that I would go to Africa someday to do missions work. But then again, I did not personally know any mission agencies nor any missionaries to ask for advice.

"Where do I start? How do I start?" were my big questions.

CHAPTER 1: A HUMBLE BEGINNING AND CHILDHOOD MEMORIES

Perhaps the better question to ask was, "Why me Lord?"

My humble beginning is an illustration of how the Word of the Lord is true in my life. I was literally the weakest child in my family. My parents did not even think I could grow up to be a healthy person. Even I, myself, did not think that I could travel to far-away places because as a child I had serious motion sickness – even on a one-hour ride to another city. Truly it is only by the Lord's grace and power that I could do what He has called me to do.

I grew up in a family in a very small town called Pasig in the eastern part of Metro Manila, the capital city of the Philippines. (Metro Manila is in Luzon, one of the three main islands in the Philippines: Luzon, Visayas, and Mindanao). I was born breach one morning in July of 1968, in Batangas, a province south of Metro Manila. According to my mother, the local midwife struggled so much trying to help her deliver the baby (me), that finally the midwife sent my mother to the hospital. With the help of the doctors, I was turned around and delivered properly. I thank the Lord that even at birth His hand was upon me.

I remember that my parents struggled to make a living to provide for their big family. My mother was already a widow with five children when my father met her. They got married and had more children, including me. I am the third child of four daughters of Floresto and Fortunata. Just like other blended families we had challenges and complications.

However, I grew up as a normal child who loved to play. I have fond memories of playing with my sisters Cecil, Tess, Fey, Carol, and other children from the neighborhood.

When I was around five or six, however, I became a bit frail in health. I loved to play but I got tired easily. After a little bit of running and playing catch or "hide and seek," I remember feeling so tired that I would stop and just sit on the sidelines and watch my sisters and other children continue playing. At that time, my mother became concerned about my poor health condition, which doctors said was anemia. My mother did her best with limited resources to give me the nutrition my small body needed. She encouraged me to eat green vegetables, liver, and other nutritious foods, which I didn't enjoy much. Now, looking back, I am very grateful to the Lord for blessing me with a loving and caring mother who even made me a supplement, a yeast powder drink with honey that tasted awful – but I guess it helped me.

When I was 6, I saw some of my friends in the neighborhood going to school. All my older sisters went to school every day. Because I had started learning to count at age four or five and had learned the simple *ABCs*, I was eager to go to school, too. But at that time, with our family's economic status, going to a kindergarten in a private school was a real luxury.

Finally, when I turned seven, I was excited that I could go to the first grade[i] in a public school. It did not take long for me to catch up with my classmates who had previously been to kindergarten. I thank the Lord for Mrs. Frias, a good and patient teacher. I liked reading, and in just a few months, I was amazed that I could read sentences and short stories in English and Filipino!

Unfortunately, because of my health issues, there were many days when I was unable to go to school. I do not remember how I passed the quarterly school tests. I think I barely "made it." At the end of my first school year, I remember the day when my mother and I got my report card. My first-grade teacher spoke to my mother and said something like, "I understand your daughter has some health issues, but I think she is good and smart; she can make it." Talk about the mercy of the Lord! It must have been one of my first tastes of His mercy.

At the end of second grade, Pasig Public Elementary School, where I attended, had a major reconstruction. The first to third graders were moved to another location in town, which made it farther for me to commute. So, just prior to entering third grade, my parents decided to transfer me to a nearer public school in our community, Dr. Sixto Antonio Elementary School, (DSAES). Just like any other kid in a new school with a new environment, I did not feel comfortable at the beginning, but it did not take long for me to become friends with other girls in the school.

In the last quarter of third grade another illness struck me. For a few days I was throwing-up a lot and unable to eat. I was hospitalized for two or three days. The doctor told my mother, "If you had not brought her that soon she could have died of dehydration." I saw the hand of God again protecting and taking care of me.

In fourth grade, I continued to enjoy playing with new friends at school. In fifth grade, I started to learn to ride a bicycle with friends. I soon noticed that my health was improving.

When I was around 10 or 11 years old, however, my father lost his job with a Chinese company. I remember that he had already worked in a factory in our town for a few years. I do not remember other details, but I remember he had a big change of job. He started working with a company that provided custom brokerage for imported items. This new job actually provided us with a few years of better living conditions which resulted in better health for me. I also improved my academic skills. In sixth grade I joined sports and played volleyball, which I continued through high school and college.

Since I had better health, it was a lot of fun to be able to play like a normal child. During weekends and summer vacations[ii], I would go out and play with my classmates and friends as soon as I finished helping my mother with morning housework. My friends and I had fun climbing trees, playing hide and seek and other fun games. When I saw the sun go down, I knew it was time to go home, get cleaned up and ready for supper.

The Turning Point

When I turned 13 or 14, I started to have questions in life. I had questions such as "Who am I?" "What is my purpose?" "What is the meaning of life?" "Who is God?" "Is He real?" and other questions for which I did not know where to find answers. In the middle of my high school years, political and economic disturbances in the country hit my father's job.

In my senior year of high school, a series of personal crises led me to give my heart to the Lord Jesus. As I was growing up, my family devoutly practiced Catholicism. I remember that when I was very small, my mother used to bring me to the church. I always knew that there was a God who created everything. I prayed to Him but did not know or understand that Jesus is the only way to God the Father. One evening, I came home from school activities a bit later than usual. I was about to walk to our apartment when a neighbor saw me and invited me to her house. She had invited me in the past, but I was not interested. That night, I was feeling "low" because of many concerns about school and my future.

For three years in high school,[iii] I had tried to keep good grades to stay in the top ten of our class. This achievement gave me a scholarship. I knew my family was proud of my academic achievements. In my fourth year, being aware it was my last year of high school, I thought I could have fun. I heard college life would be serious and not much fun. So, I joined some fun extra-curricular activities such as playing volleyball on the varsity team, participating in reserve military training, and hanging out more with my friends. The result was that I neglected my academic studies. A month before high school graduation, one of my teachers called me for a meeting and discussed her concerns about my academic performance. It was like a wake-up call. She advised me to do my best on the final tests. I realized if I didn't do well with my grades, I might lose my chance to get a scholarship for college. Besides, I did not want to disappoint my parents. They were already struggling to make ends meet. So, on my way back home after school that day, I was feeling very low, and I did not know what to do. I felt like I was hitting a brick wall. In desperation, I whispered something in my heart: "God if you are there, please help me, I need you. I do not know what to do."

When my neighbor invited me to come to a Bible Study that night, I said, "Yes." At the end of the study, when the pastor asked who wanted to receive Jesus, I found myself at the altar. I clearly remember the night of February 14, 1985 when Christ came into my heart. I felt an overwhelming sense of joy and peace! I then told the Lord, "I give you all my concerns – whatever happens, I will be fine." I felt peace and had faith that God would take care of me. I found meaning and purpose in life through the Lord Jesus Christ. I realized Jesus is the answer to my questions in life. I started reading the Bible also. In the past, I had tried to read the Bible, but I had a hard time understanding the stories. Since Jesus came into my heart, I felt the Bible became more alive and interesting. There were still questions in understanding the Bible. However, as I personally read the Bible, attended Bible studies and church, I gained more understanding of it.

God also gave me my first miracle – concerning my school academics. To my surprise, at graduation I received the second highest honor among all the senior students. I was awarded salutatorian! I truly praised the Lord for His mercy.

With the grace of the Lord, I was able to go to university through a scholarship I received because of my high school academic standing. When, during the latter years in my college, I was not able to keep my scholarship, my mother and older sister Fey supported me to finish my accounting degree.

When I accepted Jesus into my heart and started to have a personal relationship with Him, a lot of things started changing inside of me. I now had peace and hope. I felt the sense of guilt was gone because I knew God had forgiven me of my sins.

During my college years, however, I struggled with my Christian walk. I was not consistent about going to church or reading the Bible. I did not know how to be a Christian. My family was not happy that I had changed religions--which was how they perceived my change of church affiliation. I felt alone and misunderstood.

Finally, in my senior year of university, a turning point came in my life. One Sunday during the church service the preacher prayed for us to receive the baptism of the Holy Spirit. I felt for the first time, the awesome presence of the Lord. It's like He came down from heaven and touched me. I realized God is so holy and pure, and I was an unworthy sinner. But then I felt like His love just wrapped around me. I came down to my knees, sobbed for a long time as I felt the weight of His glory. It was then that I made a commitment to serve and follow Jesus wholeheartedly. This old hymn became an anthem of my soul.

> "Take my life, and let it be
> Consecrated Lord to Thee,
> Take my moments and my days,
> Let them flow in ceaseless praise."

When I made that decision to follow the Lord Jesus Christ, I did not realize just how much it would change my relationship with my earthly father, as well. Even though my parents did not have a great marriage, I remember having a good relationship with my father when I was younger. He was always proud of me because I was the only child in the family who was consistently at the top of her class. I often brought home medals and trophies from contests in science, essay writing and other academic competitions. One time my father bought me a very beautiful and expensive bicycle that nobody else in the neighborhood had. It was a gift for graduating from elementary school with the highest honors as valedictorian! I knew he was proud of me.

A Conflict and the Power to Forgive

"Forgive us our sins, for we also forgive everyone who sins against us..." (Luke 11:4 NIV)

As I mentioned above, things changed between my father and me after I started going to a born-again Christian church. My father decided that I had become hooked on a new religion. He thought that I had lost my mind. A series of conflicts grew between us until we reached an impasse.

I was still young and immature. I did not understand then why my father was so upset about my being very involved in a new church. I also did not understand that my father was himself going through a rough time with the loss of his job. To help with the family's economic situation, my mother had moved to Australia to work to support the family. Then one day, we were all shocked when we learned that my father had been diagnosed with stage-four lung cancer.

My father was in and out of the hospital. One day the doctor told my mother and older sister that there was nothing more they could do. The doctor said that maybe he could have another six months to live, so we brought him home. Early one morning, as I was preparing to go to work, I felt a nudge in my spirit to pray for my father. I felt the Lord speak these words in my spirit, "Call a brother in the church to pray for your father." I almost argued with God. "But Lord, I am hurting." The Lord said, "But you have to forgive."

So, with tears in my eyes, I knelt down next to my bed and asked God to help me forgive my father. After work that same day, Brother Jun from my church came to visit my father. They talked for an hour, but I did not join their conversation. After that visit, Brother Jun told me that my father, with tears in his eyes, had prayed to accept Jesus into his heart! I was so thrilled and happy that my father finally gave his life to Jesus!

However, a week later, my father passed away. It had been only a month since he had been diagnosed with cancer.

A month after my father passed away, I went through an intense emotional and spiritual struggle. It was more than natural grieving. I was overwhelmed with thoughts of his untimely death. My father had accepted Jesus only a week before he passed away. I had been hoping for a miracle from the Lord to heal my father so that he could testify for God and we could find healing in our relationship.

That was the hardest part of grieving: the thought that God did not answer my request. After talking to God, I felt I heard Him say that because He loved my earthly father, He wanted to take my father to be with Him. So instead of feeling bad and being bitter against God because of the death of my father, I began to be thankful that God had helped my father get to heaven sooner to spare him from further suffering.

After I got settled with the Lord on the issue of my father's death, I thought my life would be fine with smooth sailing. I had now finished college and had a good job in an excellent company. I was holding a full-time job in a big company that owned a large chain of department stores in the Philippines in the cost-accounting section. I was also involved with ministry in the church, and I thought I could now be more focused on serving the Lord. My life seemed to be perfect, or so I thought.

At that time, being in my early twenties, I could have pursued further education and had a career in the corporate world. An office co-worker and I talked about small business plans with a food franchise.

However, a few months after my father passed away, in 1992, I felt a restlessness in my spirit. Amid the many hours I gave to serving the Lord in the church through various ministries, I still felt there was something stirring in my heart. I worked with the children, young adults, and youth ministries; I visited families in their homes. I loved going out with the team doing evangelism and outreach. I was also involved with church administration and bookkeeping.

The Lord also gave me the opportunity to have a Bible Study in the company where I worked. It all started when one or two of my officemates asked me about God and my faith. Initially, we started a small Bible study group of three to five people. Then workers from other departments joined us. In a few months we grew from three people to fifteen who met once a week. Others moved to different jobs, but new ones came. The Lord did amazing things as I saw lives change; some of them started going to a Bible-believing church.

Going back to the prayer room at the Prayer Mountain where I felt God speak to me about going into missions, I asked Him, "Where do I start and how do I start?" Still in the prayer room, I heard God speak, "Go to a seminary, I will instruct you further."

I started to look for ways to prepare myself. I inquired about different Bible schools and seminaries. I found a Bible college near my workplace. At first, I thought I could continue my job during the day and go to Bible college at night. So, I enrolled in that Bible college. However, I did not have peace in my heart. I realized that it was not the way the Lord was leading me.

I felt the Lord was asking me to give up my job and trust Him to provide. I asked Him again, "Lord how will I support myself? How will my family understand that you are calling me?" At that time, I was the only born-again Christian in my family.

When I tried to speak with my mother and my older sister about the possibility of leaving my job and doing seminary studies to serve full time in church work, they both expressed a hint of disapproval. They thought I would waste my university degree by doing full-time work in the church.

I took my family's disapproval as an indication that maybe it was not the right time yet. For a few months I tried to resist the Lord's nudging. I pretended to be fine until things began to not go well with my job. I was losing my joy and peace. A couple of times I almost had road accidents while going to work. Finally, I realized there was no way I could run away from the Lord's calling.

In December 1992, I turned in my resignation to my work supervisor, effective January 1993. It was difficult to explain my resignation to some of my officemates, and even to some of my friends, but the hardest of all was trying to explain to my family and relatives. The Lord, however, helped me get through it. (After some years, my sister and her husband accepted Jesus as Lord and Savior and became my ministry partners.)

"Hundred Islands" is part of the 7,100 + islands in the Philippines

CHAPTER 2: TRYING TO RUN AWAY LIKE JONAH

But Jonah arose to flee to Tarshish from the presence of the LORD… (Jonah 1:3)

Now the word of the LORD came to Jonah the second time… (Jonah 3:1)

In January of 1993, after I had resigned from my secular job, I was all excited to begin a new chapter of serving the Lord full time. Our church leadership was happy to have me working as church administrator of a small place we had found to rent. It doubled as a church office and a place for mid-week activities. On Sundays, our church rented a room in a nearby government building.

I was not aware that the one most unhappy with my going full time to serve the Lord was the devil himself. He tried his best to discourage me from fulfilling the calling of the Lord Jesus in my life.

I was part of the team which pioneered our church. We had gone through a lot of challenges and difficulties in starting it, so I thought that we had already weathered any possible storms. In its third year, however, something happened suddenly that almost tore the church apart. It took about five years for the church to recover. More than half of the church members left after the senior pastor resigned. I did not understand what had happened, and it nearly broke me to see the church almost fall apart. I thought I had made a big mistake leaving my job to serve the Lord full time through the church.

I tried to find a part-time job in accounting as a freelancer. A couple of companies were interested in hiring me. However, they asked if I could do "double recording," meaning to have two sets of records so they could avoid paying taxes. I refused to comply. I did not want to compromise my faith in that kind of job.

The thought of going to a seminary kept coming back to me. Again, I was faced with the question of how to find a seminary and afford tuition. In the meantime, I tutored students and became a substitute for a staff member who was on leave from the university from which I had graduated.

One time, I found a book with stories about a Christian worker who went to China and met many persecuted Christians. Another time, I watched a very interesting movie about China. Both instances caught my attention and whetted my interest in the country of China.

Occasionally I went to a big church in another city which sometimes had guest speakers from the United States of America because the founding pastor was a missionary from the USA.

One mid-week service had a larger attendance than usual. I found out that the seminary which shared the building in which the church was housed had a special event. There was a guest preacher from the United States of America.

The preacher looked like he was in his 50s, a big man with silver hair, who preached powerfully. I found out later that his name was Dr. Lamar Vest, who used to be the General Overseer of the Church of God World Missions in Tennessee. I don't remember the main message, but it was something about missions and the needs in China. Towards the end, he gave a strong challenge. I still remember his words, which went something like this, "All of you who are 25 years old and below, I want you all to come to the altar. I want you all to take the challenge to serve God on the missions field."

His words were imperative. He did not say, "Those who want to go to the mission field, please come." He said, "All of you who are 25 years old and below, just come." He said it three times. I was in the back pew, talking to myself. "No, not me!" But he said 25 years old and below. I thought, "I will turn 25 years old in two months from now. Does that mean, I should go to the altar? Lord, no, not me!" The preacher kept calling, "Who is 25 years old and below here? Raise your hand!" "I can't lie," I told myself. "Come down here!" The preacher kept calling.

"I'm coming," I told the Lord. "but it doesn't mean I am going to missions." I tried to forget about the spark in my heart for missions to serve God. The wound from the incident at the church was still fresh. I did not understand why some people who were dear to my heart in the church had to leave. I realized how young I was in the faith that incidents like that could shake me.

When I got to the front of the church, the altar was filled with young people who were praying, crying, and asking God to touch them. I felt something warm touch my cold heart. I found myself crying, asking God to forgive me for running away from His calling. The old preacher started to pray with a loud, thick, southern-American accent for all of us to be used by God in missions. Then he mentioned something about the need in China. I left the building with a renewed heart. I was still talking to the Lord. "Yes, Lord, I will obey!"

CHAPTER 3: A FRESH START

Being confident of this very thing, that he who has begun a good work in you will perform it until the day of Jesus Christ. (Philippians 1:6)

I continued serving in the church, doing administrative work. However, I started to be less involved, especially in teaching children and young people. Somehow this made me think I was not in the best spiritual condition.

One time I was sharing with one of the church leaders about my idea of getting trained to be a missionary. He shared with me possibilities for short-term training for pastors and local missionaries, but I told him that I was interested in going to a seminary. From our conversation, I felt like he was not excited for me to go to a seminary, but that was exactly what I thought the Lord was telling me to do.

One day as I walked down the hallway of the same building, I met another pastor whom I knew. He told me he was taking a class in the seminary which was in the very same building. It seemed like a light bulb flashed in my head. I asked the pastor, "Where is it? How do I inquire about some programs in the seminary?"

Finally, in June of 1993, a full year later, I heard the Lord telling me clearly about missions and going to a seminary, so I enrolled at the Asian Seminary of Christian Ministries (ASCM) in the program of Master of Divinity with a major in missions. A new chapter in my life began. I met new people and started to have new friends.

I was excited about the lessons I enjoyed with the best instructors in the seminary: Church History in Asia, Writing Class, Theology of the Holy Spirit, and other courses. The seminary was small enough that everybody knew each other. Though I was one of the new students in the master's program, I felt welcomed by the other students.

One person at ASCM who left an impression on my young mind was one of the professors named Dr. Barnes. I saw Dr. Barnes at the seminary when I came to enroll for the first time. I had just finished all the paperwork for enrollment and was about to leave the building when I saw an older gentleman come sliding down the banister from the second floor. I was a bit surprised and found it quite amusing to see a silver-haired man, with his white dress shirt, black pants, and socks without shoes, playfully sliding down the banister. He saw me and introduced himself. I told him I was a new enrollee. He said he was happy to meet me and handed me a coin – a one-peso coin.[iv] I thought it was strange, but I accepted it. Later, I found out that he loved to give one-peso coins randomly to students.

As I got to know the students, staff, and professors at ASCM better, I found out that Dr. Barnes was teaching Basic Doctrine and other classes in the bachelor's program. Although I did not have a chance to take any of his classes, I saw that he was very caring and kind to everyone he knew in the seminary. In his seventies, he was very dedicated to the Lord and to teaching young students. He was funny, too. There were times when I saw him doing battle with some flies in the cafeteria. Well, I understood. Who likes flies flying around? Armed with only a rubber band, he managed to kill quite a few of the pesky flies.

Whenever he had challenges with getting his missionary visa, I heard Dr. Barnes say something like, "When I become president of the Philippines, the first thing I will do is to sort out the immigration office!"

One time, as I was sitting at my desk in the office, Dr. Barnes came and asked for something. Then he stood next to a wooden pillar and started rubbing his back on the corner of the pillar. He started to tell me, "Do you know that today my Norma has now been with the Lord for twelve years, three months, and five days?" I was stunned and did not know what to say. I later heard that he often said something like that to someone almost every day. I was touched by his love and dedication to his deceased wife.

A few years later, I heard that Dr. Barnes was in the hospital and very ill. Accompanied by other friends from the seminary, I visited him in the hospital. Even though he looked weak, he still recognized us and managed to say some encouraging words. I will never forget his words to us, "Thank you for coming. Did you know that you did not have to come? Even if you had not come, the Lord knows your heart. It is the intent of your heart to see me that matters to me."

I did not know that it would be the last time for me to see him in this lifetime. A few days later, the staff and students of ASCM had a special memorial service for this man who had touched so many lives. Many of the old and current students poured into the venue on that day to pay tribute to Dr. Barnes. Everybody was blessed and felt loved by him. ASCM named the library after Dr. Barnes in honor of his service to the seminary for so many years. His dedication to serve the Lord left an impression on my young mind, especially knowing that Dr. Barnes served the Lord past retirement age and died on the mission field.

ASCM is also the place where I joined a small group who met and prayed regularly for missions. They were talking about the nations of China, Indonesia, the Muslim world, and other unreached people groups.[v] I had no idea about those topics, and so I came to almost all the weekly meetings and listened with great eagerness. I saw and read a lot of material about unreached nations and unreached people groups. In one of the mission classes, our professor, Dr. Miguel Alvarez, gave us a project to organize a mission conference around what was called the 10/40 Window.[vi] This is an area in the world where the least evangelized people are located, including such regions as Asia, Africa, and the Middle East. Many in those areas follow the religions of Islam, Hinduism, Buddhism, and others. It was sad to know there are still many people in the world who have not heard about the love of God and the Gospel. The 10/40 Window mission conference was well attended by Christians from other churches who had an interest in missions. We also invited well-known church leaders and experienced missionaries from different mission agencies. A few years later, some of my classmates went to other countries as missionaries: to India, Indonesia, China, Japan, and other places.

My friends and classmates knew my interest then was in the nation of China. My growing interest led me to know and research more about the huge country which the world knew little about at that time. I was amazed to discover that, in fact, it is the most populous nation in the whole world, and that one out of every four people in the world is Chinese.

I learned that Christians are being persecuted in China. I then remembered the book I had read and the movie I had watched on the same subject. I continually went to the small mission prayer meetings and started to get to know other students. We soon became good friends. As I regularly attended the Friday prayer time, I began to hear more news about China from other sources as well and became more and more interested in missions.

At the same time, I also had some prejudices against the culture and tradition of the Chinese people in the Philippines. I heard that some Chinese businessmen in the Philippines were shrewd and successful but seemed not to be treating their employees with fairness. In addition, I heard that Chinese could only marry other Chinese. At that time,

I only knew the Chinese who lived in the Philippines as I had not met Chinese from Mainland China. I did not know the difference between the overseas Chinese and the mainland Chinese. (Later on, I met some Chinese friends in the Mainland who were kind, generous and hospitable.) With my prejudice against Chinese, plus the stories I had read about missions to Africa, I was more interested in going to Africa. One time, I bought a cassette tape of songs about missions in Africa. I had not even opened the tape yet when it got lost! I thought the Lord was saying, "I did not tell you to go there." (I still have not found the cassette tape to this day, by the way).

I argued, "But, Lord, I do not like the Chinese!"

One time I woke up from a very clear dream. I was in a large house that was very dark. I heard a woman screaming. I remember the words clearly, "Bu yao, bu yao!" When I woke up from my dream, I had no clue what the words meant. Later I found out that those words were actual words in Chinese and meant, "I do not want, I do not want!" (At this time, I had not even started gaining Chinese language skills).

After about two semesters in the seminary, the seminary president, Dr. Miguel Alvarez, who had a big heart for missions in Asia, opened a program for China missions. Dr. Miguel Alvarez is a missionary from Honduras to the Philippines with Church of God World Missions. He has been a big influence in my life with mission work. My good friend in the class, Marissa, was working on development of a curriculum for the Chinese Studies Program. She knew I had a strong interest in China missions, so she recommended me to be hired as the program coordinator for the Chinese Studies Program.

Together we worked on the curriculum, hired qualified teachers and facilitators, and recruited some students for the program. We had about thirty students for the six-month program. We studied culture, history, and basic Chinese language. I gained more understanding of China as I took the class while working as the program coordinator. At the end of the program, six of us from the class went to China for an exposure trip.

It was my first time to raise funds for a mission trip. A thousand dollars (about 25,000 pesos at that time) was a big amount for any Filipino. It was also my first time to put together a mission trip. I was stretched to the limit as I put the team together, connected with the right people inside China, and at the same time raised funds! Dr. Charles Quinley was one of my professors in the seminary class. I was very surprised when he gave me a big amount. He said something like this: "I don't usually give to short term missions, but I think God has something for you on this mission trip."

I praise and thank the Lord for providing through the help of many different people!

CHAPTER 4: THE FIRST TRIP!

Have I not commanded you? Be strong and of good courage; do not be afraid, nor be dismayed, for the Lord your God is with you wherever you go. (Joshua 1:9)

At the Border

In June of 1995, we boarded a plane from Manila to Hong Kong, together with five other Filipinos from the China Studies class. We were four single women and two married men. I thank God for a pastor who helped me organize the trip and gave me some contacts who helped us go into Hong Kong and from there into the Mainland. I also thank God for friends who prayed for me and for people I did not even know who helped with the funding for the trip.

Our team of six people stayed with some friends that they knew. I was introduced to the family of Mr. Moses. They were from the USA but had lived in Hong Kong for many years. He arranged for our team to meet some contacts in the Mainland. Again, I was thankful to the Lord for the kindness of those Christian workers who accommodated us and helped us throughout the trip even though they hardly knew us. They helped us to have some basic orientation and guidelines for going into the Mainland.

After about a week, we got our visa to enter the Mainland. Mr. Moses, his son-in-law Chris, and our team of six from the Philippines all traveled together. We all crossed the island of Hong Kong into the Mainland by taking about a one-hour train ride to the border. I saw many people crossing the border in and out. After clearing through immigration, we walked over a small wooden bridge, linking the province of Guangdong and Hong Kong. Crossing the border, we took a two-hour bus ride to an airport. Then we took a plane from Guangdong airport to another city in the southwestern part of China.

The First Entry into the Mainland

After almost three hours in the air, our plane landed in the capital city of a very large and populous province in the southwestern part of the country. The small, old airport was in the middle of a farm field. As we walked down the stairs of the plane into the open air, I felt the warm breeze of a late June summer. When we walked outside the arrival area, there were many men and women who swarmed us. It almost scared me as some of them were yelling and aggressive. I did not understand what they were saying in Chinese. Our team leader, Mr. Moses, knew the city well as he had travelled there frequently. He also spoke the language well. He told us, those men and women following us were "hawkers" offering taxi rides to the city. After some bargaining, we finally got a taxi ride. As we drove along the road from the airport, I saw many rice fields and small mud brick houses.

When we arrived in the city, it looked gloomy but laid-back. There were thousands of people riding their bicycles and cycle rickshaws on the streets. The roads looked run-down and there were many tall, old tenement buildings. I observed that this city looked very different from a city in the Philippines. In the Philippines, most people live in individual houses, whether small or big. In that city, I noticed most people lived in seven-story tenements. I did not see any individual houses except in the countryside or rural areas, where they had small mud-brick houses.

Our team arrived in the middle of the city and checked into a small one-star hotel or hostel where a lot of tourists and back-packers stay. We had a good supper, and after a long day of crossing the border from Hong Kong and flight to the city, we all had a good evening of rest. The following day, we walked along a road where we saw some old men sitting on chairs in an outdoor barbershop while someone cut their hair. There were many vendors along the roads selling fruit, vegetables, meat, spices, plastic plates, and other wares. There were some small shops selling steam buns, noodles, and other cooked food. The air was filled with pungent odors from all kinds of spices and food. I also noticed that most of the signage was in the Chinese script. I heard people talking loudly and yelling in the street. Unfortunately, I did not understand any of the words they were saying.

We were met by two women who were Christian workers from another Asian country, Ana and Ming. They were excited to meet us as there were not many mission teams that came during that time. In fact, there were very few foreigners visiting the country. Consequently, most of the time the handful of tall, white-looking people would 'stand out' in the crowd. Ana and Ming gave us a tour of the city and a college campus. There was only a handful of local

Christians in the city of 6 million people, and we had the privilege of meeting some of them. Those believers were very discreet about letting other Chinese know that they were Christians, even more so, to associate with foreigners. When we visited their homes, we were therefore very careful not to draw attention to ourselves. When we were in public places, such as restaurants, we were careful about how we prayed and how we talked. During meals, we prayed with our eyes open. We were told that as tourists in the country, we were being carefully watched. I was told that phone conversations were monitored as well as tourist comings-and-goings in the hotels. It was a real challenge to be normal tourists in that country.

One memorable visit we had was with an elderly Christian lady. Two of us on our team traveled with our host to the northwestern side of the city. We walked down a small dark alley until we arrived at an old tenement building. We were careful and discreet as we entered a small apartment in that old building. We were met by two women: an older lady and her daughter. We called the older lady Sister Liu. Sister Liu looked like she was, perhaps, in her late sixties. Though she looked old, she was still strong and had clear eyesight. She was short, had silvery hair, yet still had a lovely face, radiant with a beautiful smile. I noticed that she stooped a bit. I found out through an interpreter that she and her husband were survivors of the Cultural Revolution.[vii] Her husband was a Christian leader and had been sent to a labor camp in the 1960s. While her husband was in prison she suffered from humiliation and persecution because of their faith. According to Sister Liu, there was a time when she was forced to go to the public square in their town wearing a wooden signboard around her neck. On the wooden signboard something was written to humiliate her and her family, something like being a traitor or having committed treason against her country. She and other people with her had to stand in the public square with signboards on them for several hours.

As we talked, she mentioned that when the leader of the nation (Chairman M) passed away in the mid-1970s, the new government issued a policy to release the prisoners who were very old or sick. About ten years later, after twenty years of imprisonment in the labor camp, her husband was finally released. By that time, her husband was old and very sick. He passed away shortly after he was released from prison. I also met her middle-aged daughter who was the leader of a small group of Christians who were meeting secretly.

Our team then visited a college campus where we met some students. Two of them were young women who had already been introduced to the Christian faith but had not yet made a decision. (After some years, I saw those two young ladies become Christians). I heard that in most schools, they were taught that there is no God, and that religion is not good.

Culture, Culture

We were also introduced to some of the delicacies of that province, which was known for its great food and spices. They had hot pepper called *wajiao* or numbing pepper in English. A tiny bite would give your whole mouth and face a numb feeling because it was very spicy! They had *wajiao* and *lajiao* (numbing pepper and chili pepper) in most of the food they served. Food became one of my major adjustments. Being new in that culture, I did not acquire a taste for that kind of spice until many years later. We also enjoyed a variety of local food with stir-fried vegetables, tofu (bean curd), meat, noodles, steam buns, rice, and other dishes.

Adventure in a Mountain City and the First Train Trip

Another memorable part of the trip was our excursion to a mountain city in that same province. We split the team into two groups. My team consisted of two men from the Philippines, an American named Chris, and Ming. The rest of the team stayed in the city with Ana, while Moses returned to Hong Kong. My team took a long bus ride to a mountain city in the west. I was told the bus ride would take about 10 to 12 hours through winding mountain roads. I enjoyed the ride from the city through the rugged mountain roads into the countryside. From the bus, I could enjoy the scenery: the big, beautiful mountains, green and lush trees, and a wild river running down the side of the mountain. There were a lot of sharp curves and steep hills with deep ravines on either side.

As the ride got longer and longer, the road became rougher and more rugged. The small bus, which looked old and filthy inside, was packed with local people who were transporting their big bags and sacks of food and grains. As we passed through the narrow roads between the mountain and that wild river, every time we met another bus or truck on the narrow road, I prayed, "Lord don't let us fall into the pit, into the river, or off the cliff."

We stopped a couple of times on the road for meals and "potty" breaks. The already eight-hour bus ride was getting longer and longer for me. I noticed a change in elevation, and I started to feel lightheaded. We were driving up to six to seven thousand feet above sea level.

When I was a small child, I remember that I could not travel long distances during most of our family trips because I got car sick. For some miraculous reason, the Lord sustained me on that very long trip at high elevation. A couple of times during the long bus ride we were stopped by some policemen on the road for checks and inspection. I was very nervous during check points as I had some Christian materials in my backpack. According to Ming, our team leader, distribution of Christian materials was not allowed in that country. I was also told a week before that trip that there was a foreign Christian worker who had been caught bringing in some Christian materials. Ming said that when someone is caught carrying and delivering Christian materials, if they are a local person, they could be put in jail. If the person is a foreigner, they will be asked to leave the country immediately. In some cases, they could be banned from coming back to the country for a certain period. I felt uncomfortable and very nervous when I heard this news. I prayed a lot during the trip.

Every time an officer entered the bus and inspected everybody, I prayed quietly, "Lord don't let them see the Christian materials in my bag."

After the long ride, we were told that the road to our destination was blocked due to heavy rain and flooding. The driver took a different route and we ended up staying in a small town nestled on the top of the mountains for the night.

The following day, after almost 24 hours of travel, we reached our destination, of eight thousand feet above sea level. The mountains were gorgeous, and some were covered with snow. The town, however, was flooded and there were lots of fallen trees and washed-out roads. I saw that a small bridge had been damaged by the flood. Many people were on the road. I saw a crew of news reporters from a local TV station. People on the road kept staring at us, as we were the only strangers in the city. I'm sure they noticed that we had a white American with us on our team.

I noticed that the people in that mountain city did not look like the Chinese I had seen on the Mainland. I was told they were mostly from an indigenous group in that area, a people group called Tibetans.[viii] Tibetans looked bigger in build than the

Chinese and their skin was darker. They wore different clothing, spoke a different language, and looked more like native Americans than Chinese. Some of the men had long hair, wore leather hats, and had knives strapped onto their belts. The women wore long heavy robes with wool lining. Their hair was long, and some was braided with beautiful and colorful ornaments of turquoise and orange stones.

I saw a lot of the older men and women carrying prayer beads and prayer wheels, which are small pieces of metal they constantly spin in their hands while they chant endlessly to their traditional idols. We checked into a hotel, the only hotel in the city, and the only nice-looking building. I was told it was a government-run hotel.

I was relieved that the other team members delivered the Christian materials we brought to a local church. Since Ming was careful not to attract the attention of watching authorities, she brought only two people on this errand. Chris and I waited in our assigned hotel rooms. While at the hotel waiting for the errand to be completed, I got a little nervous and uncomfortable. Chris knocked on my door and told me that a man came to his room and spoke with him in Chinese. Since he did not understand Chinese, he did not know what to do. Neither did I know what to do. So, we both sat down in the hotel lobby waiting for the rest of the team. While sitting in the lobby, we noticed a strange looking Chinese man who sat across from us. He sat there obviously watching us the whole time. When our friends arrived after visiting a local Christian, we felt relieved. According to Ming, it was possible that someone from the hotel staff or a government worker was there to keep an eye on us as visiting foreigners.

The following day in the morning, our team visited a temple, as part of our cultural study. Even though the city was very tightly managed by the local Han Chinese, most of the people were Tibetans. They still practiced the traditional religion of worshipping idols. I saw some old temples, pagodas, shrines, and altars just outside the city. A young Christian girl accompanied us to one of the temples. Our team of five went to the temple and saw all kinds of false gods and idols, small and big. A lot of them were colorful but looked grotesque. We saw young men wearing long red robes, praying to their idols. There were local people, too, and some old men and women with prayer beads and prayer wheels. They walked around the temple while chanting. When we got out of the temple, I saw the young Christian girl, our tour guide, still waiting for us just outside the gate of the temple. I was told through translation that some local Christians did not feel comfortable going inside a temple associated with false gods, most of which were grotesque-looking idols. Some local Christians also think that the worship of idols could be associated with spiritual oppression.

In the afternoon, Ming decided to visit another local Christian in the town. I had the opportunity to go with her and was excited to meet a local Christian. We walked on a narrow road at the back of the hotel and passed by some buildings and houses. We went to an old house that had a second floor. I heard that they used the second floor as a meeting hall for the small church. We were greeted by an older gentleman and his wife who prepared a good meal for us. Ming had a long talk and shared many things with them. I did not understand much since the conversation was in Chinese. While they were having a serious conversation, I kept looking out of the window, enjoying the scenery of far-away, tall mountains. A couple of times, I noticed a man in a green uniform, walking up and down on the road, whom I thought was probably a policeman. When I spotted him, I became concerned and whispered to Ming, "Sister, there is a policeman on the road!" We both stood pressed against the wall next to a big window to hide as we looked down the road. I knew Ming was concerned about danger for our local host family if they were seen with foreigners. I was a bit nervous during the whole visit, praying for the Lord to protect us.

When we got back to our hotel, it was almost dark, and I felt relieved to be back. I was even more relieved when we returned to the Mainland the following day. I thanked the Lord that the travel back to the big city was shorter and better than the trip going up! There were a couple of roadblocks due to landslides, but after a 12-hour bus ride, we reached the main city.

Our first 18-hour train ride to visit other cities was significant, too. I had no clue how it would be. When we got to the train station, I was shocked by the sheer number of people traveling. It was summertime and there were thousands of people lined up together with their big bags of rice, produce, and all sorts of things. I had never seen anything like it before. Most of those traveling were peasants and were still wearing blue tattered Mao suits.[ix] They looked like scattered sheep without a shepherd.

At the train station, we queued along with the thousands of other people moving toward the main gate to board the train. When the gate opened, everyone ran toward the gate and there was chaos everywhere. Everyone pushed and shoved. I thought I'd be crushed. It was the wildest thing I had ever seen! I almost missed the train. As hundreds of people ran in different directions, I lost some of our team members. I did not know which direction they went. Suddenly, I recognized a tall white man sticking out in the middle of the crowd. I knew it was Chris, our team member, so I followed him. When we got in front of a door of the train, we could not find familiar faces nor anyone from our team. The train looked very long with many car numbers and doors. I had never ridden a long-distance train at that point in my life. In the Philippines we usually rode buses or cars for long distance travel. So, I did not know that the train tickets had designated car numbers and seat numbers for each passenger. Besides, I did not know how to read the Chinese script on the ticket. Neither Chris nor I knew what to do when we could not find our team members. Suddenly, we heard a big loud whistle and we both understood the train was about to leave. We almost panicked as we looked around to find some of our team members. Thankfully, I recognized a voice in the crowd, running toward us, yelling, "Vicki, Chris, this way!"

We realized we were waiting at the wrong platform. We saw our friend Julie, the Chinese girl who had volunteered to go with us. We ran as fast as we could since we realized our car and door entrance were at the other side of the train. I thank the Lord we were not left behind!

When our team got to Beijing, the capital city of China, I noticed that the people and way of life were a bit different from the culture in the rural and suburban cities we had visited. Just like most large cities, people were more urbanized and better educated. There were more tall buildings, bigger and wider roads, more cars, and varied kinds of transportation. There were more bicycles and more traffic jams on the road. I noticed, however, that the people there and in other urban places that we visited in China seemed indifferent, cold, and a bit unfriendly. They were competitive and seemed to have a defensive attitude. I felt in my spirit that people in the whole country had a sense of emptiness and a lack of purpose in life. For a lot of them, it seemed life was just one of existence and survival.

Being Asian myself, I had thought China would not be much different from the Philippines. A big difference, however, was the language. During that time, in the mid-1990s, I hardly met anyone who spoke English, even in most of the big cities. Most of the public signage was also in Chinese script. Another big difference was hygiene, something people didn't seem to care much about. It was common to see people spit anywhere and a lot of men smoked in public places.

I enjoyed the trip for the most part, however, except for the hygiene issues in public places. Anyway, the Lord did an amazing job for us all on the whole trip. He provided everything we needed, and He made a way for us to meet significant people and to see what we needed to see.

Capital city in the northeast

A busy train station in the northeast

CHAPTER 5: MORE PREPARATION AND MISSION TRAINING

I will instruct you and teach you in the way you should go; I will guide you with My eye.
(Psalm 32:8)

Our team of six flew back to the Philippines after the three-week-long trip. I knew then in my heart that the Lord was calling me to China. Right after I came back from that trip, the Asian Center for Missions (ACM) in Manila, officially launched a full training program to equip missionaries for service in Thailand, India, and China. It seemed to me to be a clear signal to enroll in training for China ministry. I decided to quit my job at the seminary as the assistant to the president and at the same time, I dropped my seminary classes. I was a young person and thought it was the right thing to do. Looking back, I wish I had finished my seminary training. The ACM mission training consisted of six months of full-time, intensive training. Without any support from my own home church or family, I plunged in with just faith that God would provide.

The Lord was faithful and provided so that I could finish the program without a job or financial support. I remember a time when someone gave me a large pizza for lunch when I did not have lunch money. Another time someone gave me his extra lunch. He had no idea why he brought extra food for lunch that day. God provided for me in different and amazing ways.

I was one of twenty-five students being trained, some of whom were housed by the organization because they came from far-away provinces. We had fun in the class, and we were like one big family. We learned a lot from our teachers and instructors who were mostly missionaries or involved in missions. We had lessons on the History of Missions, Cross-cultural Considerations, How to Preach, Missionary Life (my favorite), How to do Spiritual Warfare, Research and Planning, Spiritual Formation, and other lessons which would prepare us for the mission field.

Part of the program was a trip to the country for which we had registered. There were three teams. One went to Thailand, another to India, and my team went to China. There were seven of us on the China team. Again, the Lord provided everything from the plane ticket to accommodations and food.

The Second Trip

Before our team left from Manila, I started to have fears and struggled with the Lord. Though I had already been to China and knew the Lord was leading me, still my flesh wrestled with obedience. The realization hit me: "What if God was seriously calling me to China?" I began to worry about my future and my life. I was only twenty-seven years old at the time; I thought I was still young to give up my future plans and life to serve God in China. I heard some comments that some single women in the mission field become *old maids*. As a young single woman, the thought of *not getting married* scared me a bit. I had hopes and dreams of a future with my own family – husband and children. I was having second thoughts about going with the team. I asked a friend in the seminary, Mrs. Sonya Moral, to pray for me. After she prayed for me, I felt peace and regained strength to proceed with the trip.

Just like on my first trip, we settled in Hong Kong for a week. ACM made all the arrangements for us to connect with a mission organization in Hong Kong. It was a big relief for me since I had made most of the arrangements myself during the first trip. Our team went to five cities on the Mainland. Three of them were places I had visited during my first trip.

The Heart of God

One time while in the prayer room of the apartment where our team stayed in Hong Kong, I asked the Lord again, "Lord if you are really calling me to China, allow me to feel your heart for the people of China." I felt like Gideon in the book of Judges when he asked certain things from the Lord about fleeces on the ground to confirm that the Lord was really calling him to defend Israel from their enemies (Judges 6:36-40). Now, I was asking for a definite sign, too.

The following day while our team was praying together, I felt something warm fall on my head. Then, I felt something sharp in my heart. It was more than a physical pain. I knew it was not a heart attack. It was a deep pain in my spirit that I could not explain. I began to groan and weep as my heart felt like it was being pierced. I had experienced the pain of losing a parent and the pain of being heartbroken from a relationship, but this was a far deeper pain. I felt the Lord spoke to me saying, "This is how my heart breaks for the people in China, because they are deprived of knowing me." I wept and wept, not for myself, but for the heart of God for China.

Adventure at the Border, Train Rides, and Historical Tours

After more than a week, our team finally received our visa to enter the Mainland. Part of the training from our host group in Hong Kong was to send us on a day trip to the Mainland to bring some materials across the border for the Christians. We were a team of seven from ACM. With the guidance of an experienced missionary, Matthew, we were instructed to pack our bags with Chinese Bibles and teaching materials. We were told to be very careful and discreet in order not to draw any attention to ourselves. We were encouraged to pray a lot and rely on the Holy Spirit for guidance. At the border between the island of Hong Kong and the Mainland, our team walked quietly and followed the long line of people who were crossing the border. I carried a big black duffle bag. At the border, I saw that every person had to go through a scanner with an officer watching. I saw our team leader walk through the line and pass through the scanner safely. I was very nervous and quietly prayed a lot, asking the Lord what to do. I was hoping to hear the Holy Spirit speak loudly and clearly what to do.

When my turn came to pass the scanner, I put the heavy bag in the scanner hoping the guard would not see what was inside. Nervously, I laid the big bag on the scanner belt, but just in time, the guard suddenly stood up and walked away. I picked up the big bag hurriedly at the other side of the scanner and walked away as quickly as I could. Half a minute after I had picked up the bag, the officer came back to his seat and just let me pass through without any questions. I was walking away from the scanner when I heard the guard say something in Chinese. I thought he was calling me back. I looked back and saw another foreigner passing through the scanner who was being asked about his bag. I was not sure what was going on since I did not understand the language at that time. I hurriedly walked away. At the other side of the bridge, on the Mainland side, our team gathered together. We were all rejoicing and thanking the Lord that we passed safely, having crossed the border with our materials.

We delivered all the materials to a safe place from which they would be given to some local Christians. At that time, in the mid-1990s, Bibles and other teaching materials were rare. Local Christians did not have access to those materials. I was told that the man next to me in the scanner was caught with Christian materials. I was told that if somebody were caught, they could be penalized with a fine, and the materials might be confiscated. Three years after this incident, I heard news from friends that our tour guide Matthew, the missionary who had led us, was caught with a bag full of Christian materials in a train station in the Mainland. According to some friends, the penalty for him was that his passport was stamped *blacklisted* for five years, meaning he was not allowed to enter the Mainland for five years.

Our team went to the key cities in the north, south, and southwest. We had fun riding long hours on the train and on buses. The longest trip was a train ride from Guangzhou to Beijing, which was 49 hours long. (Now, the trip only takes about 24 hours with the fast train.)

During my first trip, I was able to see some important historical places like the Great Wall of China and the Forbidden City. I thank the Lord that, together with the ACM team, I was able to visit again these important historical and cultural sites on that second trip. Both historical sites were in the northern part of the country, in the capital city of Beijing. It was a privilege to see the rich culture and history of the country. Our team enjoyed climbing a part of the Great Wall which was open to tourists. It was a very long and tall wall with steep steps. The Great Wall was originally built as a fortress and protection from invading enemies. Different parts of the wall were built in various places during different periods from 2nd to 7th century BCE. Our team spent almost two hours of climbing to reach the peak.

The Forbidden City is the palace museum of the emperors during the different dynasties in the country. It was fascinating to see the huge palace with many rooms displaying ornate oriental designs. According to the tour guide, there were close to eight hundred rooms in the palace. There were also several large ancient mansions for the families, workers, and servants of the former emperors from Ming to Qing Dynasty (1420-1912). It was called the Forbidden City because the common people were not allowed to go inside the gated community or the palace.

The Lord once again provided people and contacts for us to visit. We were able to gather information for our required study and research on the culture. This information would be used in planning our long-term mission. We thanked God for His provision for the whole trip and for the people He allowed us to meet along the way. On the second trip, I felt I was more prepared because I knew what to expect.

Back to Manila and Graduation

Three weeks into the trip, all three teams from China, Thailand, and India returned to Manila. We came back to the training classes and shared our experiences. Everyone had amazing stories to share. Most of us were excited to finish our training and return to our intended countries for long-term missions.

After two more months, graduation finally came. In February 1996, all twenty-five of us finished one of the first ACM Missions Training Programs. We finally finished our intensive classes – eight hours a day, five days a week, for six months. There was a big celebration with all the ACM officers, staff, supporters, families, and churches of the graduates. We were all commissioned to go and make disciples of the nations we had been praying for. The main speaker was Mr. Gordon Robertson of Christian Broadcasting Network (CBN) who obeyed the call of God to missions when he first came to the Philippines from the USA with his family. Together with Dr. Alvarez, Mr. Robertson started the Asian Center for Mission.

Entrance to Forbidden City Palace

CHAPTER 6: THE WAITING

I waited patiently for the Lord; And He inclined to me and heard my cry. (Psalm 40:1)

After our Missions Training Program, the various teams in our class were all excited to start planning for long-term strategies to reach our intended countries. I paired up with two ladies who shared my heart to reach out to the university students and young people of Beijing (the capital city of China). Flor, Gina, and I pulled our research together and looked for different ways to find an open door into the city of Beijing.

Our other main consideration was resources. After the training, we were now expected to raise our support and have our home churches send us off. Before I took the training program, I had been at the small church I helped pioneer. The church, at that time, was still recovering from the crisis mentioned earlier. When I told the pastor in charge about my heart for missions, I suppose it was understandable that it was not something the church could be concerned about at that time.

With the encouragement of my friends in the seminary, the Lord led me to another church where I became the church accountant and met new people. Everyone was welcoming and friendly. The church is now called Lighthouse Christian Community in Alabang, a city south of Manila.

The founder and senior pastor at that time was my professor in the seminary, Dr. Chuck Quinley, who, along with his wife and six children was a missionary from the United States. From the time I went on my first trip to China he had been supportive of me.

I sent an application to a language institution in Beijing. While waiting for a response, I continued my accounting work at Lighthouse. I had made new friends and had become a full-time employee. In fact, I spent most of my time at the church. With my father already gone, my mother in Australia, and all my siblings having their own families, the church became my family.

Months came and went but I still did not get a response from the institution to which I had applied for language studies in Beijing. I had also sent an application to an organization that hired English teachers for China. After some time, they replied and said that since I was not a native English speaker, I needed a master's degree in teaching English. As that door closed, my pastor encouraged me to keep waiting while serving in our church through various ministries.

While waiting, I kept praying earnestly for the Lord to open a door for me, but I became impatient. As months turned into a year, I was about to give up. I accepted that maybe it was not yet time. "Waiting" is truly a difficult place to be.

I soon realized that I should just enjoy life and my service in the church while waiting. I got involved with various ministries (Bible studies, outreach to women and children, youth, and young adults) while working as the church accountant.

During this time of waiting, I got distracted again with thoughts of being in a relationship and having a family in the future. Did I have to surrender that desire to the Lord and consider it as part of the sacrifice to obey God's call in my life? Did obeying God mean relinquishing the possibility of being in a relationship just to keep my focus on God's calling? It was very difficult. I struggled with my personal desires and reconsidered the thought of going to China as a missionary. However, though the flesh was weak, the Spirit of God in me strengthened me to overcome my temptations and fears.

He Made a Way When There Seemed to Be No Way

In August 1996, I saw an advertisement for cheap airline tickets to Hong Kong. My mother was visiting the Philippines from Australia for a few months. I asked her if she would like to travel with me to Hong Kong to get a "buy one, get one ticket" promotion. I told her I had friends in Hong Kong we could stay with. Under normal circumstances, my mother would not spend much money for a vacation since she was usually prudent with her finances.

For some reason (the Lord's intervention), however, my mother agreed and traveled with me to

Hong Kong. We stayed with my friend in Hong Kong, and I showed mother around the city. While there, I ran into Ana, the missionary I had met during my first trip to China. I had lost contact with her. At that time email and Facebook were non-existent. I did not expect to see her in Hong Kong at that time. She found out that I was still waiting for responses to my applications in China. She then offered to help me apply to a college for language study in the same city in the southwestern part of China where I had gone during my first trip. I felt excited about it even though I was still hoping I could get an entry to Beijing.

Before I left Hong Kong, my hopes were renewed. My mother was happy to meet Ana, and she was at peace that I would be with her. After some time, I received the application papers and I returned them immediately.

I waited for a few more months. Before the end of 1996, I got a response from Ana. My application to the language institution was in process! She advised me to start preparing. As I did this, my application for funding from Word for the World Christian Fellowship got approved. I am thankful for Dr. Alvarez who recommended me to be supported by this church. I am thankful also for the faithful support of my home church, Lighthouse Christian Community.

I was told that to go to the mission field, I should have at least 20 prayer partners. So, I started working on my first prayer letter. I sent copies to my friends and asked them to pray.

Ana advised me to be ready to travel in time for spring classes. Around December, my very good friend from the seminary, Li, came back from a three-month mission trip with a mercy ship called the MV Doulos. She told me she would like to go to China with me. I was excited the Lord was putting things together and funds started to arrive!

By January 1997, I started to look for my replacement at the church and worked on finishing the year-end accounting. I still did not know who would take my place, but I knew I had to leave by mid-February. With the Lord's grace, I finished my work at the church, sent prayer letters, and raised the funds. On top of that, I had to be part of the entourage at a friend's wedding. Finally, by the end of January, the Lord sent a wonderful accountant, Mrs. De Villa, to replace me at the church. It was amazing how fast the Lord worked everything out after almost two years of preparation and waiting!

One day in the very first week of February, my friend Li and I boarded a plane to Hong Kong. After almost two weeks in Hong Kong waiting for our visas and papers to be processed, we crossed the border into China. Together with Li and Ana, we flew to the same city in southwestern China that I had visited on my first trip. Little did I know on that first trip that this very place would become my second home for ten years.

When we entered the crowded, noisy halls of the airport, I heard a woman screaming, and then I saw a tall, lean Chinese man in a green uniform dragging her away. I was terrified, not knowing what was happening. A few minutes later, Ana explained to us that the woman was caught stealing or committing some other infraction of the law. It was a very memorable and traumatic introduction to the Mainland for my long-term mission work.

After more than two hours of flight, our plane landed at the small rustic-looking airport where I came during my first trip. There were many people and tourists at the airport. Again, many *hawkers* and *scalpers* swarmed us offering taxi rides or a car for hire.

We boarded a taxi and drove through the countryside. I noticed a big change in the climate. The weather was chilly because we had arrived at the end of winter. I was already wearing a couple of thick jackets. Coming from a tropical country like the Philippines, I was not used to cold weather. The sky looked bleak and cloudy. As our taxi drove along the road, I saw rows of half-mast flags all over the city. I found out it was the day the whole country was mourning the death of the leader of the country, Chairman Deng, the man who had opened China to the world in the 1980s. The end of his leadership in the country was the day when my many years of life in China were to begin.

CHAPTER 7: A NEW CHAPTER BEGINS

Go therefore and make disciples of all the nations, baptizing them in the name of the Father and of the Son and of the Holy Spirit, teaching them to observe all things that I have commanded you; and lo, I am with you always, even to the end of the age. (Matthew 28:19-20)

Culture Shock and Adjustments

"Lord, did you really call me? Did You make a big mistake?" I asked the Lord as I struggled during the first few months of adjustment. As I remembered my cross-cultural training back in the Philippines, I thought I knew what I would be going through. I should have known that classroom training is different from actual experience. I was learning a new language which was totally different from both my native Filipino language and English. In fact, I heard from some friends that Mandarin is one of the most difficult languages in the world to learn.

My friend Li and I enrolled at a local college to study Mandarin (Putonghua), which is the national language of the country. I learned that there are fifty-five officially recognized ethnic minority groups[x] in the country in addition to the Han majority. Each of the groups has its own language and culture. The national language of the country – Mandarin or Putonghua – in English means, "common language." China is currently the most populous country in the world, with almost 1.4 billion people. The time I first came to China in the mid-1990s it was known to have

1.2 billion people. About 90% of the population speak Mandarin. Although each of the fifty-five people groups has its own language, all people are expected by the society to at least understand Mandarin. In most cases, people in the big cities or those who have been to school are expected to be able to speak Mandarin. Additionally, each province or region, has a local dialect.

The local college we attended had many "ethnic" students from nearby towns. Our friend, Ana, helped us to get connected to the college. She knew the college and the city well. She translated for us and helped us understand the people and the culture. As a language student, we stayed in a dormitory for foreign students and studied separately from the local Chinese students. I met other foreigners from different countries who were also studying Chinese. I was not sure who among the students were Christians or businessmen.

I learned that Christian workers were very discreet and careful, as they did not want to attract attention from officials, who were not open to Christianity.

A major adjustment for us was living in another culture, which made almost everything different. The food was even distinct from the Chinese food I knew back home in my country. The southwestern cuisine is well known for its hot and spicy taste. Yes, it is very spicy food! The province is especially known for hot peppers called *wa-jiao* or numbing peppers as I mentioned earlier. The food tastes good but is spicy and greasy. Later, the Lord gave me grace, and I acquired a taste for the food.

Another adjustment was the big difference in the temperature. I was used to the tropical weather in the Philippines, around 30 degrees Celsius (85 degrees F) every day, except on rainy days. In the Philippines there are only two seasons, dry and rainy, but China has four seasons. I happened to arrive in the middle of winter when the temperature was usually 5-10 degrees Celsius (40-50 degrees F). There was no central heating system like they have in the northern region. I just had a small space heater, that I moved around in the room so I could stay warm. In the early mornings, when it was still dark and very cold, I had my prayer time under layers of blankets! That was the first winter of my life in a cold and damp place where the sun usually does not shine. It was cloudy or foggy almost every day. I was not aware of "weather depression" – how a cloudy day can affect one's mood. I did not remember "adjusting to very cold weather" as being part of my cross-cultural training! I struggled, wearing layers of clothes, in my attempt to stay warm.

Living quarters were another major adjustment. Since we were staying in a college dormitory, we used a common bathroom and kitchen. The building was very old and not well-maintained. At night, I had to go to the end of the hallway for the toilet. There were no individual shower stalls – only a big common shower room in the middle of the building. The hot water came only twice a day, one hour at noon and one hour at 5:00

p.m. Twice I was in the middle of a shower when the hot water ran out. So, I ended up rinsing with cold water! It was necessary but not fun wearing layers of clothes: an undershirt, a sweater, and an overcoat. With the addition of underpants and heavy outer pants, knitted hat, scarf and winter gloves, I felt like a Panda bear walking around!

I missed my family and friends. For the first time I knew what it meant to be "homesick." The strange thing with this "sickness" was that I did not know what medicine to take! Back in the Philippines, the last few years before I moved to China, my life and work centered mostly around the church. After my father passed away, in my mid-20s, I was basically living by myself. My mother, at that time, lived in Australia and my siblings had their own families. So, I was usually with my friends in the seminary or the church, where I worked full time. In my first few months in China, I missed my church family terribly. Being in a new country, I struggled with whom to make friends. I soon discovered that in this new place, church life was totally different. I did not see church buildings like we have in the Philippines where almost every town had churches of various denominations. In my Chinese city, I did not see any church buildings except for several traditional temples where idols were worshiped. There was also one Muslim mosque in the city.

Our small team, Li and Ana and I, gathered on Sunday mornings for worship and Bible study. We met in one of our dormitory rooms and sang quietly. We were careful not to attract the attention of the neighbors. I was always careful and afraid. I was concerned that someone might ask if I were a Christian and discover that I was a missionary. I was concerned, too, that the police might come and see us and arrest us. Later, either on Saturday afternoons or Sunday afternoons, three to four Chinese joined our small group. I came to know that in that city there were very few Christians – only a handful. So, I missed my church in the Philippines where we had about one hundred people inside a nice building, with a worship band, a program, and a full sermon from our pastor. Later, I learned that a small number of local Christians in the city met secretly as small groups in their apartments. They were called "house church" meetings. I also learned that there was a registered church in the city – a government-recognized church. According to some local believers, many Christians were not comfortable going to the registered church which met in a building because they thought the church was regulated by government officials. As years went by, more and more house churches, or small groups, grew as new believers multiplied.

During difficult times of adjustment, the Lord taught me an important lesson, that I could not "do it on my own." The Lord broke through my independence and taught me to depend more on Him. He also helped me see my weakness and some attitudes that needed to be changed. Yet through all the difficulties and challenges of adjusting to a new place, the Lord was faithful to see me through. His Word in the Bible became very real to me. *"And He said to me, 'My grace is sufficient for you, for My strength is made perfect in weakness.'" (2 Corinthians 12:9)*

Here are some excerpts from my early journal entries, in which I share some of the challenges, joys, and triumphs during my first few months of adjustment. The Lord was gracious and merciful through it all.

March 10, 1997
This is only my third week in this land. I think I have seen street fights five times already. I have noticed hostility among the people here; it seems they do not have love and respect for each other...One time I saw a woman being beaten in the market, and another time in a store. Today, right here at the university dormitory, I saw another fight. Of all the people, this older lady, we call her "Ayi" (ayi means aunt in Chinese and is a polite way to address an elderly lady), had a fight with another worker. Dear Lord, please pour out your love in this place. A lot of things have already happened to Li and me. Her new bicycle was stolen the other day! "Lord, help me pray for this place." (My new bicycle was also stolen a week later.)

March 11, 1997
I have gathered some information. I found out the minority people of China (indigenous groups) have some privileges. The majority group is called Han which composes about 80-90% of the population. I found out that in school, the students who are from the minority groups have lower qualifications and requirements for passing grades. With minority families, they are allowed to have two children, while the Han have a one-child policy[xi]... I am also praying for an open door to have friends among the Chinese students.

March 18, 1997
Lord, to you alone I can pour out my heart. It seems I am beginning to feel the pain of culture shock and adjustment in this place. Much as I do not want to complain, however, I know it will not be good if I just keep it inside of me. I don't want to just burst later. It seems trivial, but it is starting to pile up...The weather is usually cloudy. I hardly see the sun, so the cold weather of 10 degrees is very cold for me. And the hot shower time is inconsistent. The major thing, I guess, is the difficulty in communicating – the language stress! On top of that is the stress with the formal language studies. Besides that, most of the facilities in the university are inconvenient. It is difficult, but I'm trying to be okay! I also try to endure the bathroom and "squatty potty"(hole in the ground) toilet which is also for common use of all the tenants in the dorm. Friendship is also a challenge. I do not know how to talk with other people, other than my two friends. I am not sure what to say, what not to say, and how much to say. I do not know whom to trust and whom not to trust. "Father, I know You have called me. I feel like I cannot complain to anyone, even to my church or family, because I know I asked you for this. However, I have to face the reality that we have a difficult situation here. I am starting to feel the loneliness and longing for family and friends. I am waiting for letters from friends. I still thank you that I am starting to make some friends here even though it is difficult to communicate. I hope you understand me. It is also difficult to dress up in the morning. I get stressed out with putting on layers as it is still freezing cold for me. It is a good thing that the

classroom is just walking distance away. Please help me, Lord, to get used to this place and to get adjusted to this new life. I know that your grace is sufficient."

Little Breakthroughs

After a couple of months adjusting to new weather, a new culture, a new language, a new life, and a new season, the Lord with His grace and mercy started to give us some encouragement. My friend Li and I began to make new friends on the campus. I learned that many of the young Chinese students were eager to learn English. As we both studied and lived on the campus, we met many students. We also learned about campus life. Early morning, when it was still dark and cold, we heard the loud noise of the wake-up call through the campus radio or megaphone. Every morning we heard the words "Yi! Er! San!" spoken very loudly between 5:00 and 6:00 a.m. In English, it's "One! Two! Three!" The call signals for the students to gather in the campus square for their early morning exercises. After fifteen minutes or so of physical exercise, we heard their national anthem. Next, we heard a bunch of words in Chinese that we did not understand. I later learned that most words were political propaganda or some announcements from school or the government. After the morning exercises, I heard all the students run to the cafeteria and line up for breakfast. By 7:30 or 8:00 a.m. they were in their classrooms to begin their classes. Before 8:00 a.m., I also ran to my Chinese class. I thank the Lord that by riding my bicycle, I could get to my classroom in 5 minutes.

Every day, my friend Li, four students from Korea, and I had four classes: Reading, Listening, Writing, and Speaking Chinese.

More of my journal entries:

> *April 1, 1997*
> *Hello Dad, (I called God, "Dad") A lot of things happened again. Last Sunday (March 23rd), my Christian friends and I here went to another college campus. We visited a Yi family (Chinese Minority people group), who are good friends of Ken and his family. (Ken is a new believer, and his wife is a growing Christian too). The family prepared a lot of food for us. Then we went for a short hike on a little hill. The trail wound up in an open field, with flowers and vegetable plants. It was a beautiful and peaceful place. We played and went kite flying. It was a happy day!*
>
> *The past week, we were also busy with the Easter Celebration (which is not a holiday in this country). We prepared a meal in the dorm for the workers. Joanne, No, and Ana's friend, Sandy, came also. After dinner, we played some games. We had fun! Last Sunday we had a small gathering for local Christians. About 10 people came, and a young lady accepted the Lord. Julie, according to a friend, had heard the Gospel from others over a period of 10 years. After those 10 years she finally made a decision to believe in God. It was a joy for us all to witness her big decision! (A big decision, especially for an atheist.) Then in the afternoon, Ana, Li, and I prepared another Easter program for our*

language teachers in the college. All our teachers and their families came. We sang some songs, and Ana shared the meaning of Easter (in Chinese). We played some games and had fun. I noticed most of them are good singers. Even if it was just for a game, they sang with all their hearts. For most of our language teachers, that was their first introduction to an Easter event. It was our discreet way of sharing our faith, since Easter is not a recognized holiday in the country.

April 5, 1997
Today we went bowling with single Chinese friends. It was fun even though it was a bit pricy for my budget. We also had a good Bible study. I praise the Father, I am happy, He is good! I am now experiencing His abundant grace. In my weaknesses and shortcomings, He has made me feel His overflowing love.

April 9, 1997
I am sick today with stomach flu and feeling very weak. While physically resting I took time to study the Bible. I read a quote that says, "Those who wait patiently for the timing of God have nothing to fear or be envious about." My devotional study was on "waiting,"

April 15, 1997
This morning, I was late for class. I didn't study last night. I caught a cold because of the cold shower last night. I went to the public bathroom, thinking it was the time for a hot shower. Right in the middle of my shower, the hot water ran out. So, I rinsed myself with

the freezing cold water right in the middle of an early, chilly, spring evening! I thought I would die, "grr," Cold! I woke up crying to God as I cannot make it again to take the test for the Hanzi (Chinese writing). It is very difficult for me to memorize the radicals (Chinese script). I was thinking of skipping the first class, or maybe not taking the test. I am ashamed of myself because I am doing poorly in Hanzi (Chinese Writing). But then the Spirit said, "Just go." Just before I left for the first period class at 8 a.m., Gong Laoshi (Teacher Gong) called and said she couldn't come to the class. She had some problem. I felt sorry for her, but I was thankful to God I had time to study. Still the two hours were not enough. It is a pain! I can't memorize the Chinese writing. When class came, Teacher Cui moved the test until tomorrow. PTL! Thanks a lot, Dad!

April 19, 1997
Yesterday the administrative staff and the foreign students had a field trip to a city in the northwest — about three hours travel. It is the home of a minority people group called the Qiang. They have their own language and traditions. They wear traditional clothes that are colorful and not the same as the Han people. We travelled via some roads on the hills, and along some rugged mountain roads to the village nestled in a valley. We crossed a tall, hanging bridge with a river under it. It was a bit scary. Then we hiked about two kilometers to get to the village. At the entrance of the village two Qiang ladies, in their beautiful traditional clothes, welcomed us. They lit some firecrackers to welcome our group. They prepared a lot of good traditional food for us. Then we walked around the

village as the village leaders showed us around. There were some pigs and chickens around the village, and a lot of giggling children followed us. One of our college staff members was from that village. After completing his studies, he was able to help his village improve their livelihood. A lot of people, young and old, welcomed us because they were curious to see foreigners. In the village square, I saw an old tower about 10 feet tall. According to the village elders, the tower is about 900 years old, built of mud and stone. An intensity 7.0 earthquake struck the village some years ago. There was some serious damage, but the tower stood strong. It is now the pride of the village. It is like their symbol of refuge and strength. Their thinking was, if the tower were ruined, their lives would also fall and crumble. We also had the opportunity to visit homes. The place was surprisingly neat and clean, compared to the lack of hygiene in the big city. The village also seemed to be quiet and peaceful.

Towards afternoon, after the long visit in the village, our group said our thanks and said goodbye to the village leaders and the village people. While walking out of the village, we passed by an elderly man who was sitting in the village gate. He looked like a native Qiang, maybe about 70 years old. The elderly man looked curious and excited when he saw this bunch of foreigners, especially the white-looking folks. He stopped one of us, a student from New Zealand. With the help of another foreign student who translated what the elderly man was saying, I was able to understand a little bit. The elderly man was saying something like, "Are you an American? Are you a Christian? An American Christian came here a long time ago. There was a church..." Then he started to sing an Old Christian hymn (in Chinese). He kept on saying things about God, Jesus, and a Book. Then he said that the books were collected and burned during a war or revolution. He kept talking and talking. The foreign student who was translating for me tried to translate as much as he could understand. I noticed that he wanted to respond and interact with the elderly man. However, he realized that the officials of our college were right behind us. (Some of the foreign students were uncomfortable and were careful not to say something that would expose them as Christians or missionaries). The college officials were just laughing at the elderly man. Somebody even commented that he must be crazy.

We, as foreign students, also think or assume that we are highly watched by some officials especially regarding any religious involvement and activities. That scene made an impression on me. It seems that the elderly man in the village gate was like the old man in Jerusalem who sat at the temple waiting for the coming of Messiah when baby Jesus appeared. The old man in the Qiang village seemed to just be there waiting for the Christian foreigners to come back to tell of the Good news of Salvation. When the old man mentioned about having a church, Christians, and the Book, it must have been about 40 or 50 years ago. I have read stories about Bibles being burned, Christian churches being closed or torn down, and foreign missionaries being asked to leave the country. Up till now, I had only read such stories in books. But to actually hear it from a local person was amazing.

After another long trip, we made it back to our college dormitory. However, I got car sick from the road trip. Lord, I pray, please send a Christian worker to that village.

(I learned that foreigners are only allowed to work, live, or study in the main cities. In remote towns and villages, like the one we visited, foreigners are not normally allowed to stay. Some places even require special permits for foreigners just to travel or visit. A year later, God answered my prayer when I met a family who was sent to serve in that village. However, in 2008, a devastating earthquake with a magnitude of 8.0 hit the area we visited. According to some news reports, more than 69,000 people died.)

April 23, 1997
Last Sunday, Ana arrived from Hong Kong. We were all excited to return to our Bible study and regular church time. However, when we got to her apartment, we were all shocked that everything seemed in shambles. Someone had broken into her apartment. Some of her important things were stolen - jewelry, videocam, some money, and other things. We were all shocked and fearful. Thank God, that she brought her computer with her in her travels, so it was not stolen.

I am still not feeling well from my recent illness. Just the other day, we had to change rooms in the dormitory. I complain again because I haven't had my rest and am still not settled yet. It has been the third move in less than 2 months.

This same day, I got a blessing. I received a package at the new post office on campus from my mother in Australia. Praise the Lord, my Korean classmate, Meijing, went with me to help translate to claim the package at the post office. My mother had sent me some winter clothes, good lotion, chocolate bars, and lipstick. "Thank you, Lord!"

*At the same time, I was upset also about Chinese studies. I still could not catch up with the lessons. I'm struggling as I feel I am being pressed and squeezed. "Dad, my body is struggling to cope. I don't know what to do. If it is just an attitude problem, I submit it to you. Please help me." I wondered why this was happening when my body was not in good condition and our Chinese lessons were getting more difficult. Then the LORD gave me this word from 2 Samuel 24:24, "... **nor will I offer burnt offering to the Lord my God with that which costs me NOTHING.**"*

(End of Journal Entries.)

After one semester (6 months) at the college, Li and I moved to another college in the northern part of the city for language studies. The accommodations for foreign students were much better. We had our own little apartment with kitchen, living room, and bathroom. Our classes were also made to suit our level of learning.

Panda reserve in the southwest province

Camel ride with Li at a tourist park in the southwest

Learning the Language

After one year, with two semesters of four Chinese classes – Reading, Writing, Speaking, and Listening – I was excited that I was able to speak the language. Every week in the class, we tried to learn about 50 to 100 words. I was told there were about 12,000 Chinese characters or words, and an average person uses about 4,000 of them. I thought I was ready to have good conversations with some local people. Then I found out that the local people actually spoke a dialect in their day-to-day life. It is similar to Mandarin; however, there are some words that are pronounced differently. As I mentioned earlier, studying the language was a challenge for me, especially writing it. I wanted an easy or more practical way to communicate, so I focused more on learning the spoken language. I noticed some of the words we learned in the textbook were basics for survival, such as words used for shopping or buying things in the market. Besides the formal language studies, I had learned to ask people how to say things. I wanted to be able to talk with the local people about their lives. With the Lord's help I managed to speak the language and to understand by listening.

The neat thing about the Chinese language is that though people of different regions speak different languages or dialects, the writing or character script has the same meaning for all. For example, the people in the southern part of China speak Cantonese, while other provinces speak various other dialects. But when they read and write the same Chinese word, the meaning is the same. They just speak the word with different sounds, that is, the pronunciation differs.

Later, a Chinese teacher encouraged me to take his class on the ancient Chinese language. I shared with him my challenge in memorizing the Chinese characters. I could not understand why and how a Chinese character, or a stroke, would mean "such and such." Most of the local people learned to study and memorize these characters when they were five to seven years old. I was struggling to memorize without understanding. Whenever I asked one teacher why they used this or that word or how a word came to be, he usually answered with the words, *"Xi guan,"* meaning *that's the practice or the habit*. He was explaining to me that, "that's how they do things," or "that's how they say it."

So, I followed the advice of the other teacher, to study the ancient Chinese language to have understanding. This class is not normally offered to the foreign students, but with the teacher's permission, I attended the local college class. Though I struggled to understand the lectures, I managed to understand a bit. I learned that the language evolved through different generations. I only took a few lessons, but it did help me to understand that Chinese characters have real meanings. The modern Chinese language is called *simplified* and the older one is called *traditional*. The original ancient Chinese characters have deeper meanings.

For example, the English word *person* or *human* in Chinese is *ren*. The character is 人 which means two legs. Another word, for example, is the word, *male person* or man; in Chinese romanization, the word is *nan ren*. The character script is 男人 which means a person in the field. In ancient times, the man usually worked in a field on a farm.

The word female or woman in Chinese is *nu ren*. The character script is 女人 which means a "person under a roof." In the ancient Chinese tradition, women usually worked inside the house while men worked in the field. When I learned the ancient meaning of the Chinese characters it helped me understand that Chinese writing is not just a bunch of chopsticks thrown into the air to make words. I gained a deeper understanding and appreciation of the beauty of the language. I wish I could have continued to study more but I did not have the time or the patience.

Later on, I heard of a book that connects the ancient Chinese script[xii] to some of the Bible stories. For example, the English word righteousness in Chinese is *Yi*. The character script is 義. There are actually two character scripts put together. The upper script is 羊 *yang* meaning *lamb* in English, and the lower script is 我 *wo* in English, meaning *me* or *I*. So, the two character scripts put together mean *lamb over me* or *yi* in Chinese meaning *righteousness* in English. In the Old Testament, the people of Israel had to offer animal sacrifices such as a *lamb* in order for their sins to be forgiven and be right with God. (See Leviticus 4:1-32 regarding sin offerings.) "If he brings a lamb as his sin offering, he shall bring a female without blemish." (v.32)

In the New Testament, as Christians, we believe Jesus became the lamb offering for the forgiveness of sin. Our righteousness is only from Jesus, the *lamb that was slain.*

"*The next day John saw Jesus coming toward him, and said, 'Behold! The Lamb of God who takes away the sin of the world!'*" *(John 1:29)*

Another word I learned in Chinese is the word *chuan* which in English is boat. The traditional character for the Chinese word *chuan* is 船. The meaning of the character is *eight mouths (people) in a vessel.* In the Biblical story of Noah's ark recorded in Genesis Chapter 6, eight people were saved by God from the flood in the ark or boat.

As I learned more of the Chinese language, I discovered that the vocabulary being used varies according to one's status in life. This means that if a person were talking with a teacher or an ordinary person, he/she would use normal life conversation. When they speak with a doctor, they use a different set of words in Chinese. When they speak with a student, they use another set of words. Since my focus was to share the Gospel and words of God, I also studied the words commonly used in Church and the Bible. The language class in the institution did not offer such lessons. I thank and praise the Lord that a local friend who had good English skills offered that class privately to some of us who were interested. I learned to say the words for *God (Shen)*, *Jesus (Yesu)*, and *love (ai)* in Chinese which helped me a lot in sharing the Gospel in their local language. *Yesu ai ni* means *Jesus loves you!*

CHAPTER 8: FOOD, COOKING, AND CULTURE!

Whatever city you enter, and they receive you, eat such things as are set before you. (Luke 10:8)

Strange Food!

In my missions training class, I learned that food is an important part of one's culture. Jesus told His disciples when He sent them out, *"Whatever city you enter, and they receive you, eat such things as are set before you" (Luke 10:8).*

With that in mind, and with the Lord's grace, I tried to eat whatever was served to me. One thing I appreciated a lot with the people in China was that they were very hospitable and generous. Chinese New Year is the biggest holiday of the year when families gather together for meals. I was blessed to have been invited to be part of their family traditions. They always gave their best meals to their guests. Chinese New Year is also the busiest time of the year when many travel to be with their families in their hometown or *lao jia*. Some shops and businesses close for a few days. I learned to stock up on grocery and food items before the holiday.

In food culture, the southwest province has been blessed with a wide variety of vegetables, fruit, and other delicious food delicacies. One of my favorite dishes was the freshly made noodles cooked in broth with vegetables and a little bit of meat. Another dish I liked had different kinds of dumplings or pot stickers. I also enjoyed all sorts of stir-fried vegetables, sweet and sour pork or chicken, *kung pao* chicken (peanut chicken), and other dishes. Since the region is known for hot and very spicy food, after a year, the Lord helped me to acquire a taste for the local cuisine of hot and spicy dishes. *Mapo* tofu, for example, is a well-known dish which is a bean curd or tofu cooked in very hot, spicy sauce which is quite tasty. I also learned one way to show appreciation to the cook for a good and delicious meal was to give a good sounding slurp. Even after many years of using chopsticks (which are used for all dishes including rice and soup), some friends still gave me comments like, "Vicki, this is the proper way to use chopsticks."

Many have asked me, "What strange food have you experienced on the mission field?" Honestly, I am thankful the Lord spared me from some of the strangest foods. Growing up in the Philippines, I know of places where some people eat meat such as frogs, alligators, deer and other animal meats. However, I came from a family where we ate usual food that is common to most people in Asia such as chicken, pork, beef, and vegetables.

One time, my friend Li and I were riding bikes on a busy street, and for some reason, we struck up a conversation with a mother and her 8-year-old daughter who were also riding bikes. In that place and time (1998), there were only a handful of foreigners in the city. I guess they were fascinated to meet other Asian foreigners for the first time. Mrs. Liu, the mom, was eager to learn English, especially for her daughter's sake. After that first encounter, they invited Li and me to visit them at their house. One time we came for dinner, and she prepared a big meal for us.

On this occasion we expected some of those hot, spicy foods. But instead, we enjoyed the normal dishes which Mrs. Liu prepared for us, such as stir-fried vegetables cooked with their special numbing peppers. As expected, most of the dishes were delicious; however, Li and I were not quite prepared for the main course that Mrs. Liu prepared for us. While the host was still busy in the kitchen, Li and I saw white looking meat in a big serving bowl. Both of us looked intently at the meat, trying to see what it was. The pieces looked too small to be chicken, and the color did not look like pork or rabbit. We had already been served rabbit meat at some other events. The dish did not look like anything we knew. Finally, our host, with a big smile, introduced her specialty, *qingwa*. I was not sure if I understood her Chinese word for that dish.

Finally, Li and I realized the special dish was *frog legs* in a spicy sauce! I do not remember much about the taste, but I thank the Lord for the spicy sauce that covered the taste and texture!

After the big dinner and a good visit with Mrs. Liu, Li and I went back to our apartment. I remember our conversation. One of us asked, "Did you see that some of the white meat still had some skin on it?" Hmm. I was not sure if I wanted to try that one again!

A Turtle Dish and a Wedding

As the end of three years in China approached, both Li and I felt led to return to the Philippines. But after seven months of rest, I felt recharged and ready to go back to China. Li felt led, on the other hand, to stay in the Philippines. In the Fall of 2000, the Lord opened a door for me to have a work visa as a bookkeeper with an International School in the same southwestern China city where I previously lived.

One weekend, one of the Chinese teachers invited me to go to her hometown for a relative's wedding. Her town was about a two-hour bus ride outside the big city. Most of the neighbors in the village were attending this wedding banquet, a big event in this small village. I did not know the couple personally, but in that culture, everyone was welcome to join in the festivities even without a formal invitation.

I sat at a table with a group of women, men, and children from the village. I guess some of them were cousins or neighbors of the bride or the groom. Traditionally, a three-day feast would be given by the families for a wedding. An average Chinese family would have 3-5 dishes for a day-to-day meal. One dish might be as simple as stir-fried onions; another dish could be tomatoes and eggs; another dish could be tofu; and still another stir-fried green, leafy vegetables like spinach or hallow-heart. Where I grew up in the Philippines, we would usually eat one meat and a vegetable dish. By contrast, especially for a special banquet meal like Chinese New Year or weddings, Chinese families would normally have a twelve-course meal!

At this wedding reception there was an assortment of meat dishes such as pork, beef, and rabbit, as well as tofu and many vegetable dishes, arrayed on the table. I learned from that experience that one of the main courses – actually a special dish for the people in this region – was turtle meat. Once again, I was grateful it was cooked in a spicy sauce. As with the other dishes, I managed to eat what was served. I remembered again the words of Jesus in Luke 10:7, "And remain in the same house, eating and drinking such things as they give…" and what I had learned from my training, just to smile and try to eat what was served.

Typically, at such a big lunch banquet, one or two women would dish some food onto my plate. That's another thing I appreciate about many of my Chinese friends – they are usually sweet and thoughtful to make sure I am eating and not being shy. They usually scoop ample amounts of food from the serving dish onto my plate.

As I have mentioned, I usually ate what was served to me. There were times when I really liked a dish; then I would ask what it was or how it was cooked. There were times I did not want to know what it was. When the turtle meat dish was served, my Chinese friend introduced it to me to make sure I understood that turtle was an exotic and expensive dish. In the middle of the meal, one of the women at the table wanted to be extra nice to a *waiguoren* (foreigner). She started to scoop the head of the poor turtle into my bowl to honor this foreign guest. When her 8-year-old son saw what his mom was about to do with the precious turtle head, he expressed his feelings candidly. They started to argue in Chinese, and I think I understood what he was saying, "Mother, I want the turtle head!"

The mom said, "No, my son, our guest should have it." When I saw the exchange, I wanted to laugh but I tried my best not to show it.

I managed to say in Chinese, "No, it's okay, let him have it." I was not just being polite, I meant it, and inside of me, I wanted to say, "Please, please, let the boy have the turtle head!" I don't remember many of the details, but I think in the end, the boy won. Whoa! What a relief! Thank You Lord, for the little boy who rescued me from having to eat a turtle head!

Other than frog legs and turtle heads, I did not have much experience with strange foods. On birthdays and Chinese New Year celebrations I was served rabbit meat. I usually felt bad that rabbits were served as a meal because I thought they were cute pets.

Cooking and Culture

In the international school, some of the teachers were fresh college graduates from the USA. We made some fun memories together as we all tried to cook in a new place with its very different culture.

Speaking of cultures, I learned from these teachers that baking is a big part of the North American cooking culture. The remote city in the southwestern part of the country where we lived didn't have the availability of imported ingredients such as cheese, butter, and other important baking items. I think, now, in the big cities, many imported cooking items are available. Many of the local people in the southwest region were not used to eating cakes, cookies, and sweet western desserts.

One of the teachers in the international school, Tiffany, was also one of my roommates. She liked to bake cakes and missed a lot of her American food. One time, she planned to bake a simple bread cake, but there were no instant cake mixes sold in the stores like in the USA. The local market had flour, eggs, and sugar, but she needed confectioners' sugar. She looked in all the stores and markets but could not find any. So, she had the brilliant idea of taking the regular white granulated sugar and bringing it to the market to grind it into powdered sugar. She had seen that some of the stores had grinders for meat or peppers, so she brought her one-pound bag of sugar to a store and asked the shopkeeper to grind it to powdered sugar. She then went to other stores to buy her vegetables. When she came back a few minutes later she took her newly ground powdered white sugar home, excited to bake her cake.

That night when I came home to our apartment, I asked how her baking experience went. She told me with a laugh that her cake turned out good except that it had the taste of *wajiao* (numbing peppers). She realized that the white sugar had been ground in a grinder which was usually used to grind the numbing peppers! She encouraged herself by saying that her sponge cake literally turned out to be a spiced cake – a good cake with the taste of spicy pepper. So, we both had a good laugh!

Cheesecake

Samantha was another teacher at the international school who was originally from the southern part of the USA. Like the other North American ladies, she also missed pies, cakes, and cheesecake. One time someone brought cream cheese to her from the USA, so she made plans to make her favorite cheesecake on that weekend. On that Saturday morning, I made plans to be home since I also wanted to learn how to make cheesecake. We gathered all our ingredients: a bag of flour, sugar, and the cream cheese. I then watched her prepare all the bowls with the baking ingredients. She put the flour in one bowl and then prepared to mix the cream cheese and the white sugar. After mixing the cream cheese and the white sugar, she tasted it, and to her surprise, it was terribly salty! She then realized the bag that she thought was sugar was actually a bag of salt! Sad to say, we both had not been able to read the Chinese label on the bag. So, "goodbye, cream cheese, goodbye, cheesecake!"

On one of my birthdays, I wanted to make spaghetti, but I did not know of any restaurant that served it. The ingredients, such as ground meat, spaghetti sauce, and noodles were not easy to find. So, I bought a chunk of beef and chopped it myself, found a can of tomato paste to make the sauce, and used Chinese noodles for the pasta.

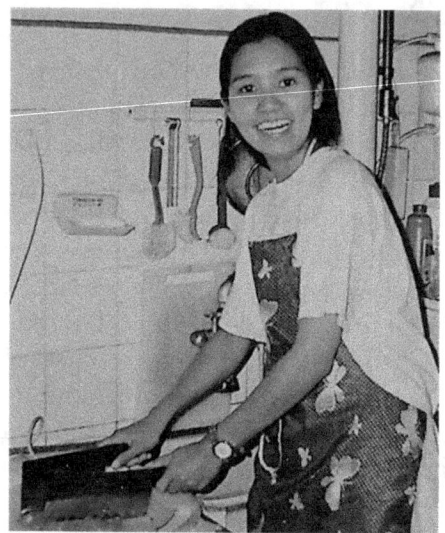

Chopping meat for spaghetti sauce

Street food - a big part of the culture in the southwest

A traditional Chinese New Year meal with a family

CHAPTER 9: SEEDS PLANTED AND LESSONS LEARNED

"So, then neither he who plants is anything, nor he who waters, but God who gives the increase." (I Corinthians 3:6)

First Adventure in a Village

After six months of Chinese studies at the college, my friend Li and I moved to a different college to continue our studies. There we visited a small outback Chinese restaurant where a young lady of about 18 worked whom we called Rachel. Rachel was excited to meet foreigners. Like a lot of the young people in the country she wanted to study English, and we were her first foreign friends. She soon started coming to our apartment. We helped her with her English lessons, and she helped us practice the Chinese language. Then on her birthday, she invited Li and me to a big dinner birthday party with her co-workers at the restaurant where she worked.

One summer, soon after that, she invited Li and me to go with her to her hometown to meet her family. Li and I were excited to meet her family and to experience local life in the country. The village was about a three to five hour bus ride outside the city. I enjoyed the countryside, because, by contrast, the city was crowded and smoggy on a lot of days. It was nice to see the hills and the green fields. I noticed a lot of the farmhouses were made of mud bricks, in contrast to the tenement buildings in the city. There was also some coal mining in the mountains.

Rachel's family was excited to meet us; it was their first time to meet foreigners. They may have been surprised that both Li and I looked Asian and were not the typical foreigners they saw on television who looked white or Caucasian. We met Rachel's father, mother, brother, sister, and grandmother, who all lived together in a farmhouse made of mud brick with a dirt floor. I noticed they did not have much furniture in the house except wooden beds, a table and chairs for eating, and a couple of benches. They cooked outside the house with a wood-burning stove made of three stones. There were chickens and ducks running around the yard. A pig pen stood at the other end of the house, and Rachel's dad was gathering some vegetable leaves and crab apples to feed the pigs.

We were served hot green tea many times during our visit. At dinnertime we were served a lot of good local dishes: stir-fried vegetables, twice-fried pork with a lot of fat, and plenty of white rice. On that visit I came to know more about the hospitality of the Chinese people. In fact, we were treated like royalty. I also discovered that in the culture of the countryside, they always serve the best to their guests, which for them is the fat of the meat. To my surprise and shock, we were served a bowl with slices of pork fat swimming in a red spicy sauce! There was no lean meat at all, just pure fat floating in a greasy, red, spicy sauce! Li and I prayed hard about our food. We were able to explain to them that as Christians it is our tradition to pray for the food. As Rachel explained this to her parents, we saw her parents just smile.

They seemed okay with it, as they also pray to their gods as religious people who worship idols. I learned that many people in the rural areas were idol worshippers while most people in the city were non-religious.

When sleeping time came, we noticed with interest that they had only one bedroom and two big wooden beds with no mattresses. They gave one bed to Li and me to share, and it seems the family all shared the bed of their grandmother. Since they did not have electricity at night, they used gas lamps. I expected that after they tucked us into bed and put up the mosquito net, the family would also go to their bed to rest. It took me a while to get to sleep. To my surprise, when I opened my eyes, I saw that the entire family was outside the mosquito net watching us (Li and me) to see how we slept!

In the morning, after we had our breakfast, I went outside for a walk. I enjoyed the scenery of the farm and fields. As I watched, I noticed members of Rachel's family coming to a small pond where they got their drinking water (the boiled water they used for tea). From the same pond, they collected water for cooking, washing their hair, and making tea. I also noticed that there was no bathroom. The ladies went to the back of the house where they washed their faces and hair. After that, they put some warm water in a small basin and used a washcloth to clean their bodies. They used a second small basin with warm water and towel to wash their feet. For toilet needs, they had a hole in the ground next to the pig pen.

That was the most challenging part of the trip for me, doing my personal business next to the pigs.

In one part of the pond, they washed their clothes. Meanwhile, at the other part of the pond, they allowed the cows and water buffalo to drink. I wished we were able to speak to them about hygiene and cleanliness concerns. However, as visitors and foreigners, we did not feel comfortable to address such issues. All-in-all, it was a memorable and interesting trip, experiencing rural Chinese life.

The visit to her family meant a lot to Rachel. We became good friends. Li and I had the opportunity to introduce her to Jesus through our Bible studies. Because she came from a traditional religious background where idols are worshipped, the story of Jesus was completely new to her. We watched the *Jesus* film with her in Chinese. One time, we think she prayed to believe and accept Jesus. Li and I continued to study the Bible with her for a few months. She even brought some of her friends to our study.

Later, Li and I went back to the Philippines for a winter break. When we came back a couple of months later, Rachel was very happy to see us. We resumed our Bible studies. One time during our study, we were surprised when Rachel told us that she believed in Jesus but still believed in the idols that her family worshipped. According to her, to be Chinese is to be a Buddhist. We realized their religion was intertwined with their culture. That was our first time to encounter something like that. Prior to that experience, we assumed that when someone prayed to accept Jesus and studied the Bible, they were already a Christian.

Later, as we got to know more about the culture and the people, we learned that some of them politely accept anything from a foreign friend, even a religion, to please that friend. We do not know what eventually happened to Rachel, because at that time our Chinese language skills were limited. Our friendship with Rachel, therefore, served as a big lesson for us in sharing the Gospel and in making disciples. We realized later that if we had introduced Rachel to a local church, she could have been discipled and could have learned the Bible in her own language. And she could have had Christian fellowship with her own people. Later, when we met other locals, after introducing them to Christ, we immediately connected them with a local church. Though we were sad about Rachel, we trusted the Lord had planted seeds of faith in her heart. Like the other young Chinese friends we met, we did not hear from her again after we left the country. Even after I returned in 2000, I was not able to re-connect with her since she had moved and changed jobs.

We also met other young students in the college with whom we had Bible studies and fellowship. However, after they graduated, most of them moved to other cities for jobs. Some went back to their hometowns. However, we prayed that our Lord had planted some seeds of the Gospel in their lives, with the hope that He would send others to water those seeds and bring forth fruit. As mentioned earlier, we also learned that it is best to partner with the local church for discipleship. We also learned the importance of **understanding the worldview of people of other cultures.** Like Rachel, many people from her culture think worshipping idols is "tied in" with their identity and nationality.

PART 2

VICKI IN THE HARVEST FIELD

Behold, I say to you, lift up your eyes and look at the fields, for they are already white for harvest! (John 4:35b)

Only Jesus

Only Jesus can save
Only Jesus can do the impossible
Only Jesus can do what no human can do
Because only Jesus can save
Only Jesus can love the way He does
Only Jesus is the Savior
Only Jesus is the King of kings
Only Jesus is Lord of lords
Only Jesus is the Almighty God
Only Jesus is the God of love
Only Jesus is the God who came from above
Only Jesus is the One who gave His life for us
Only Jesus can save our soul
Only Jesus can satisfy a hungry soul
Only Jesus can fill me up
Only Jesus is the bread of life
Only Jesus can bring lasting peace
Only Jesus can give true happiness
Only Jesus can give eternal life and bliss,
Only Jesus!

CHAPTER 10: STORIES OF FAITH AND FAITHFULNESS

The Story of Jonathan

He who loves his life will lose it, and he who hates his life in this world will keep it for eternal life. If anyone serves Me, let him follow Me; and where I am, there My servant will be also. If anyone serves Me, him My Father will honor. (John 12:25-26)

One of my favorite stories is about two young men, David and Jonathan whom Li and I met when we moved to another college for Chinese studies. David and his friend, Jonathan, were students at the same college campus. They both became Christians through their earlier friendship with other missionaries. By that time, those missionaries had moved back to their home countries. Just in time, the two young men were introduced to us. They started coming, faithfully, to our Bible studies on Friday afternoons.

One time the two young men shared with us their concern. In their college, the Communist Party representatives had started to recruit and encourage the students to become members of the Party. According to these young men, the Communist Party representatives promised them a good future, as far as getting jobs, if they were part of the party. However, they were also informed that to be part of the Communist Party, they were not supposed to be part of any religion. David and Jonathan shared with us their dilemma. As young people in a place of economic challenge, they wanted to have a bright future and the assurance of good jobs. On the other hand, the two young men had also come to know the Truth and salvation in Jesus Christ. They asked us to pray for them. Li and I wished we could tell them what to do, but we knew we had to trust the Lord to guide the young men. We encouraged them to pray and seek guidance from the Lord, and we prayed earnestly for them.

A couple of weeks later, we were surprised and delighted to hear from David and Jonathan that they chose not to join the Communist Party. We praised the Lord for the decision of the two young men to follow Jesus. I was not sure if they fully understood the implications of the big decision they had made – that if they did not join the Communist Party, their chances of getting good and stable jobs were gone. The two men continued to study the Bible with us until they finished their college studies.

When David and Jonathan graduated from college, David moved back to his hometown, a few hours away from the main city. We did not hear from him again. Jonathan went back to his hometown, too, but later came back to our city. He opened his own small store, selling electronic gadgets. We introduced Jonathan to a small group of local Christians in what we called a house church. From that time, he continued to grow in faith and in the Word. One time he came and shared with us that he felt a call to serve the Lord, but he did not know what to do. We encouraged him to pray about it and seek the Lord.

At that very time we met a married couple, Francis and Shelley, who were also Christian workers from another country. They told us of a ministry that gave Bible training in their country and wondered if Jonathan would be interested. As we all prayed about that possibility, Jonathan felt led to apply for that ministry training opportunity. The Lord opened the door for a sponsorship and scholarship. Then came the biggest challenge: how to get a visa to go to that country. During that time, in the late 1990s, it was rare for a local citizen to travel to another country. The first hurdle was to apply for a passport. In my home country, it was easy for anybody to get a passport, whether they planned to travel or not. But I learned that at that time it was not common for regular citizens to get a passport in China. I was not sure about the requirements and the process; I had just heard it was not easy. However, the Lord answered our prayers for Jonathan; he was able to get a passport and a visa. We praised and thanked the Lord. Indeed, nothing is too difficult for the Lord!

Jonathan also needed to raise some funds for travel and the cost of living. We praised the
Lord that He provided everything Jonathan needed to travel to another country and to be in ministry training.

At the time when Jonathan went to that country for training, it was also the time Li and I felt led to move back to the Philippines. As I have mentioned earlier, after almost a year of being in the Philippines, I felt led to return to the same city in China. Just in time, I heard that after a year,

Jonathan's ministry training was also completed. I was happy to know that he chose to come back to his own country because I had heard of some people who had the opportunity to go to other countries and did not return.

Later, I heard from Jonathan that he was able to resume life in China and his ministry with the house church. The Lord also blessed Jonathan with a job to support himself. Although his heart was to serve fulltime in ministry in the region, most church workers were self-supporting. It was uncommon for a church worker not to have a job or employment for several reasons. First, every adult has some kind of work or business unit that monitors them. Second, if they do not have work or a job, the community would be suspicious of them and would not understand if they say they work for a church. Third, many house churches do not have a structured system to financially support a fulltime worker.

With Jonathan, it was a joy to hear that he was able to use the Bible and ministry training he received overseas to serve the local church. During that time, the Lord also gave me a new ministry with "Aquila and Priscilla," training local church leaders and workers. Jonathan was a big help to us through translation and his understanding of the needs of the local church.

Sometime later, Jonathan was employed by yet another foreigner and obtained a good job. Later, he got married to another church leader. It was a joy to see how the Lord blessed Jonathan for his faithfulness. I felt like a mother goose who was very happy to see the couple on their wedding day.

After a year or so, Jonathan was hired by a big computer company. He and his wife continued to serve as leaders in the church while he worked a secular job which involved some local and international travel. His wife also had a fulltime job in a dental clinic. As they faithfully served together as leaders of their house church, the group gained new members and grew. Later, Jonathan got involved with another ministry which mentored and trained other church leaders. At the same time, I moved to another city for a new ministry.

In 2007, when I moved back to the Philippines, I got involved with other ministries in various places and unfortunately lost communication with my friends in the city.

In 2013, the Lord blessed me by giving me the opportunity to revisit the city and friends. I was delighted to see Jonathan and his wife again after a few years. Both continued to serve the Lord and had been blessed with a beautiful and intelligent daughter. I found out that Jonathan was still involved with ministry training and mentoring leaders not just in the big city, but countrywide. At the same time, he continued to work for the same secular company and had been blessed with a good position. He continued to have good privileges such as travel to other countries for company business.

As I look back and remember the early years of faith and choices and how the Lord had led Jonathan, I realized that when he decided to follow Christ, his life changed. I praise the Lord that Jonathan decided to follow Jesus and did not choose the offer of job security with the Communist Party. I have seen many young people his age who have had difficulties making a living. Many parents have spent thousands of dollars for their children to go overseas for higher education just to be qualified to work with big companies. In China, millions of young people are looking for good jobs. I have seen with my own eyes how the Father has taken care of Jonathan, his life, and his family as he chose to serve Him. When Jonathan was a young man in college, he had given up the offer to be part of the Communist Party and to have what they call, "a stable job in the government." Instead, Jonathan chose to follow Jesus. The life of Jonathan reminded me of the words of Jesus: "For whoever desires to save his life will lose it, but whoever loses his life for My sake and the gospel will save it. For what will it profit a man if he gains the whole world, and loses his own soul?" (Mark 8:35-36)

Currently (2021), Jonathan and his wife continue serving the Lord with a ministry of mentoring church leaders. It is an inspiration to hear that he and the church are continuing in the faith amid challenges, opposition, and persecution. He also asks prayer for safety for his family as they face threats and other challenges to their faith.

The Story of Summer

I first met Summer during one of our house church worker training events. Later, I invited her to have lunch in a western fast-food restaurant. She shared with me that she had college credentials as an eye doctor. However, in that country, whether doctors or teachers – even those working in the government – all have the same economic status. So, Summer found a job with a non-profit organization (NGO) that ran an eye clinic. Summer was a strong Christian. In fact, she started to have a small Bible study group in her apartment. She also had good English skills.

Summer had a heart to spread the Lord's Word. She continued to come to our church workers' training. She had real enthusiasm to learn and be trained to grow her small group as a house church. My co-worker Mark and I met with her on a regular basis, once or twice a month.

One time, she shared with us her frustrations with growing a church. She did not understand why some of the young people who came to her small group were not faithful to come or were not consistent. She was not sure how to help them grow in their faith. So, with once-a-month training and coaching, we tried to help Summer grow her small group as a house church. Summer was faithful to come to every meeting. At the same time, our friendship grew. There were times when I met with her personally just to encourage her as a sister in the

Lord since I understood some of her personal needs and struggles as a single young lady.

Over the course of a couple of years, it was a joy for my co-worker and me to see Summer grow in her leadership skills. It was a blessing, too, to hear how her one small group grew to become five groups. She told us that one time during a Christmas program in the church, about a hundred people came. Some of the new people accepted Christ upon hearing the Gospel for the very first time! Over the years, I saw Summer's consistency and faithfulness as she served the Lord in His kingdom. Summer continued both her job with the NGO and as a pastor who led her church which continued to grow. She also trained other leaders.

Later, I moved to other places and lost contact with my friends in that southwest city. After about seven years, in the spring of 2013, the Lord blessed me to visit that city again. I met with some friends and with Summer. At that time, she was engaged to a brother, who was also a church leader. I was so happy to see her and to meet her fiancé. As a single young lady many years before, Summer was concerned about being single and finding the right man. I saw, however, that she did not focus on that, but had faithfully continued serving her Lord and His Kingdom. After many years of waiting on the Lord, Summer, in her late 30s, finally got married to this faithful and good brother in the Lord. I was so happy to see her and to see how the Lord had rewarded her faithfulness. I heard a couple of years ago that they now have a baby. The Lord God is truly good and faithful to those who are faithful to Him!

CHAPTER 11: THE PAPER-CUT MAN

"For I am persuaded that neither death nor life, nor angels nor principalities nor powers, nor things present nor things to come, nor height nor depth, nor any other created thing, shall be able to separate us from the love of God which is in Christ Jesus our Lord." (Romans 8:38-39)

During the first year, second semester of language learning, Li and I moved to another college and were placed in the foreign student dormitory. We shared a three-bedroom apartment in the same building with an elderly couple from New Zealand who were also studying Chinese. Gray and Jessica became like parents to us. One time they told us they had a friend, Gill, who was coming to visit from England. We soon got to know Gill's big heart for the people of China. By the time Gray and Jessica went back to their country for their furlough, Li, Gill, and I had become not only good housemates, but also the best of friends.

One evening we went to the east side of the city to the night market. It was a section of the city where some sellers set up their tables and wares on the curbside of the street. There were men and women selling pottery, antique paintings, old coins, and other Chinese artifacts and trinkets. There were also shops which sold Chinese art paintings with Bible scriptures in Chinese which they knew appealed to a lot of us foreign Christians. The night art market was popular with other tourists as well.

A young man saw us and invited us to see his unique Chinese art items. These designs were made from very thin, Japanese-type white paper, on which had been colored beautifully designed art pieces of flowers, birds, and trees. When we looked closer, we realized that the designs were made of cuttings on the paper. That was my first introduction to the paper-cutting art of China. The young man, Leo, had a kind and gentle manner, different from a lot of sellers who tended to be a bit aggressive. Gill, like a nice English lady, struck up a conversation with the young man, and we all bought the paper cuts which were affordable, light, and intricately beautiful.

The following weekend, we went back to the art market and saw Leo again. After buying his products, we were invited to his apartment in a suburb on the east side of the city to meet his family. One weekend, the three of us took a taxi ride and visited Leo. He and his wife were a young couple who had just finished high school and were starting their family. Though he qualified to attend college, because of the educational system in their province, he was unable to attend. With my limited knowledge of Chinese and Leo's limited English, it was my understanding that there were quotas based on minimum qualifying scores for college entrance, and Leo did not achieve the passing score. He ended up setting up a small business which sold different items to support his wife and newborn baby. Since they could not afford to rent a decent apartment in the city, they only had a small one-room apartment with the dining area, kitchen, living room, and bedroom all-in-one. Like other Chinese, despite being economically deprived, they were still hospitable. The young couple prepared a big, nice meal for us. When they found out that their little son had the same birthday as me, we were invited later for his first birthday.

Eventually we all became good friends. Both Leo and Jane were far away from their parents who lived in other parts of the country. At that time, our Chinese language proficiency was not that good yet since it was only our second year of learning the language. We had only some basic words to carry on simple conversations. However, with the help of the Lord, even with limited language skills, we managed to communicate. Leo was a brilliant young man and was enthusiastic to learn English. Though Gill had only started learning Chinese, she was eager to talk with Leo and his wife about *Yesu* (Jesus) with translation help from Li and me. Jane was busy and distracted with the baby, but Leo was very attentive. We discovered that Leo was surprisingly interested in Christianity. He had not heard of Jesus before, or if he had, perhaps only what many people in China say, that Christianity is a western religion. However, when Gill talked to Leo about *Yesu*, she was talking to him like she was talking about a real person who she really knew, someone like her best friend! She shared that Jesus died on the cross for our sins and shared her testimony how *Yesu* had healed her some years ago from a rare disease called "Myalgic Encephalomyelitis[xiii]" (Chronic Fatigue Syndrome) or M.E. Gill's powerful testimony was that she was bedridden for a few years, but the Lord healed her from M.E. and gave her a new life in Jesus. After Leo heard the story of Gill, he prayed to receive Jesus into his heart.

A few weeks later, Gill had to return to England, but Li and I continued visiting Leo and his family and sharing some Bible lessons with him. We thanked the Lord for some bilingual Bible lessons that we had acquired. We read in English and he read in the Chinese Bible that we had found for him. Leo enthusiastically studied the Bible and grew quickly in his faith. However, his wife Jane was still not interested. We continued to be friends with her, however, and she was always sweet and kind to us. Gill, through email, always sent greetings to Leo and his wife and prayed for them continually while back in England. Leo and Jane missed Gill a lot. I missed her, too. At the end of 1999, after three years, when Li and I went back to the Philippines, the Lord provided a local house church for Leo to help him continue in his faith journey.

In the fall of 2000 when I returned to the country, I was glad and thanked the Lord for reconnecting me with old friends, both foreign and local. Leo and Jane were happy to see me again. Their son was already a growing boy, about 3-4 years old. And to my surprise they had another son! I was glad to see, first-hand, that Leo continued in his faith. He was part of a small group, often called a house church, which had about fifteen to twenty members. Leo was part of the church leadership. As his faith grew, I saw the Lord was blessing his family, too. They were able to obtain better housing, which was very helpful, especially since they now had two children.

I became busy with the job at the school and a new ministry team outreach which was led by my good friends, Aquilla and Priscilla. The local church was growing, and we saw a big need to provide workers and church leaders with some training. On a few occasions, Leo had participated in some of the training which our ministry hosted and facilitated. Whenever I had the chance, I visited Leo's family and tried to encourage his wife to be open to the Christian faith. However, she had expressed that because her family (parents) were worshippers of other gods, she felt she had to keep their traditional religion. Leo continued his faith in the Lord Jesus and his participation in the house church. As far as I knew, there was no conflict between him and his wife with regard to having different religions or faith. I think they both just loved and respected each other. For those few years, it was a joy to see their children growing.

A couple of years later, Leo and his family decided to move to another city in the northern part of the country. Leo, as a father, felt led to find a better job to provide for his growing children who needed to be in school. Occasionally they called me on the phone, or sometimes I called them. I found out he had a job with a construction company where his brother was also working.

One day, I received word that Leo was in the hospital. According to the information I received, he had been badly beaten by some men at the construction site. I did not know details, but according to his wife, he was in serious condition.

The news got out among our Christian friends (local and foreign) about his condition, and we all prayed for him. Just in time, Gill came from England to visit a city in the eastern part of China. I traveled and met her in that city. She and I prayed fervently for Leo and his family. Prayers were also lifted up for Leo by many believers.

Gill and I talked about whether we should travel and visit Leo in the hospital. At just the time we were discussing it, I heard my phone ring. It was Jane, Leo's wife. I said, "Ni hao, ni hao ma?" (Hi, how are you?)

She did not say a word; all I heard was loud and deep wailing. She wept and wept. I do not remember how long she wept and cried on the phone. I was just silent and did not know what to say when she told me that her husband had died.

About a week later, I was back in my apartment in the southwest. A bit later, Jane contacted me to tell me that she and her two sons were also back in the city. She asked me to meet with her. We all met together in an apartment. I found out that the local church, the small group where Leo used to go, had a memorial service for Leo. He was cremated in the northern city, but his remains were brought to his original hometown in the central part of the country where his parents and siblings were located. Jane felt led to come back to the city in the southwest where we lived to take care of some details.

I was able to be with Jane and her two sons for a short time. She told me they were planning to move down to Central China. The family of Leo wanted her to move there so his parents could help her raise and take care of the two sons. To my big surprise, I found out that during the memorial service at the house church, Jane had accepted Jesus into her heart. She was moved and touched by the love and care of the brothers and sisters in the Lord. Jane remembered the witness and testimony of her husband – his faith and love for God.

As we know, the Lord works in ways we do not know and understand. The death of Leo was one of the hardest and most painful experiences I had on the mission field. However, our Lord made a good thing out of that tragedy. I had no idea that through the life and death of her husband, Jane, once an idol worshipper, would come to know the One True God, Jesus Christ.

After a year or two, Jane and her two sons moved back to the same city in the northern part of the country where Leo was beaten and died. Occasionally, we talked on the phone or by email. The last time I spoke with her on the phone was in 2013 before I left Beijing. Gill, meanwhile, had shared with me that she was able to visit Jane during a trip to China in 2014. She was so happy to see Jane and her two grown-up sons. Just recently (2019), Jane sent me an email telling me that her eldest son is now in college in Beijing, and the second son is now in high school.

CHAPTER 12: SWEET FELLOWSHIP WITH JESUS AND NEW FAMILY OF FAITH

'And you shall love the LORD your God with all your heart, with all your soul, with all your mind, and with all your strength'. This is the first commandment. And the second, like it, is this: 'You shall love your neighbor as yourself.' (Mark 12:30-31)

When I finished my mission training course and was commissioned during our graduation ceremony, just like any other young novice, I was pumped up to "change the world!" Little did I know I was the one who would be changed. The Lord God in His mercy and gentle way smoothed out the rough edges in me through people and situations. I discovered there were life lessons which cannot be learned in a classroom but through real and actual experiences, like dealing with the spirit world in the mission field (Ephesians 6:12-20), adjusting to cross-cultural living, working with a team, interacting with different personalities, etc.

During my first three years in China, I had at least five friends from my home country. Because we shared a common culture and language, it was comfortable to be with them. After three years, most of them moved back to the Philippines. After that, whenever I joined an international team, I was the only one from the Philippines. Since my ministry, work, and fellowship were mostly with westerners and Chinese, I felt alone. I realized then the Lord had completely taken me out of my comfort zone so I could fully rely on Him.

I was humbled, too, that in my times of weakness, insufficiency, loneliness, and other challenges related to being a single young woman in the mission field, my sweet fellowship with Jesus had been my source of comfort, strength, and courage. I enjoyed extended times of worship and fellowship with the Lord. Through those times, I developed a closer and more intimate relationship with God as my Father, and Jesus as my best friend and constant companion. Through my sweet fellowship with Jesus, the Holy Spirit filled me with His power and strength so I could minister to others. The Lord showed me I can't give what I don't have.

Almost every year, I had to deal with visa applications and renewals. Each time our omnipotent God parted the Red Sea, as He provided visa approvals, airfare, and other expenses. He opens door that no one can shut (Revelation 3:7).

I also learned that ***Jesus' call to His harvest field*** is not just simply preaching and sharing the Gospel, it is also the blessing of knowing Him and making Him known – to know His heart that none should perish (2 Peter 3:9). I got to know more about the character of our Lord God. He has always been gracious, merciful, loving, and very patient with me. He showed me the condition of my heart and things in my attitude that needed changing (even until now). He taught me what it means to have joyful obedience, to serve Him with gladness (Psalm 100:1), instead of complaining and murmuring about inconveniences and challenges. An old hymn expresses the joy of trusting and obeying.

> *"Trust and obey*
> *for there's no other way*
> *to be happy in Jesus*
> *but to trust and obey."*

The word of God also became an anchor for my soul in times of need, fear, and other uncertainties. These verses encouraged me, *"Do not be afraid, I am your shield, your exceedingly great reward" (Genesis 15:1); "Behold, I am with you and will keep you wherever you go..." (Genesis 28:15).*

Sunday Fellowship

Besides my sweet fellowship with the Lord Jesus, I also received encouragement through fellowship with other believers. As I missed family and friends from my home country, the Lord gave me new friends and a family of faith. I heard the sayings, "No man is an island" and "There is no such thing as a lone ranger since even the Lone Ranger has Tonto." I learned the importance of fellowship with other believers, especially for young, single people. Not only was there a need for fellowship, but also for accountability, prayer, and encouragement.

On Sunday mornings, our small group of about ten to twelve people met in different apartments. Each Sunday, our group assigned someone to share a message. Sometimes, they brought a sermon from their home church on tape or CD. Another person was assigned to lead the praise and worship. At the end of the time of worship and sharing of the Word, we prayed for each other's needs. We also spoke words of encouragement to anyone in need, especially when they were going through a rough time. We welcomed newcomers and prayed for those who were moving back to their home countries. Most of us felt comfortable to share from our hearts: joys, trials, and other challenges living in a cross-cultural setting. We were like the church in the book of Acts: *"And they continued steadfastly in the apostles' doctrine and fellowship, in the breaking of bread, and in prayers" (Acts 2:42).*

After our Sunday worship service, we usually went out to a nearby restaurant and ate together. Since Sundays were rest days for most of us, we also continued to fellowship in the afternoons by playing games or watching a movie together. For each of us it was a big encouragement to be with brothers and sisters in the Lord. Even though we came from different countries, cultures, and church backgrounds, we became good friends and like family. We shared even little treasures we found in the city like cheese, butter, and other baking ingredients which were rare to find in those days. The words of Jesus to His disciples were a reality for me: *"Assuredly, I say to you, there is no one who has left house or brothers or sisters or father or mother or wife or children or lands, for My sake and the gospel's, who shall not receive a hundredfold now in this time – houses and brothers and sisters and mothers and children and lands, with persecutions – and in the age to come, eternal life." (Mark 10:29-30)*

How I miss that kind of fellowship and desire to see it in regular church services in the free world! I also learned that the church is not a building, nor an organization, nor an institution. It is the fellowship of people who share the same heart for the Lord, eat together, break bread together, pray and study the Word of God together.

During Christian holidays, like Easter, Christmas, and Thanksgiving, with limited resources available for traditional meals, we were still able to celebrate together, even though our host country did not officially recognize those holidays.

Besides fellowship and friendship, we also shared resources such as Christian materials. We also shared with one another by fundraising for whoever we knew was in need. Leaders from different Christian groups (foreign and local) promoted and organized "prayer walks" in the city and in the province. Just a few years later, we saw a change in the spiritual atmosphere with more people being open to the saving grace of Jesus in the province. I praise and thank the Lord for His power expressed through the spirit of unity as we prayed together.

As new friends came and went, they became part of my life even though I never saw most of them again. I am thankful that I am still in touch with a few who became my best friends. Even though we are thousands of miles apart, we manage to communicate. I thank the Lord for the technology of email, telephone, and social media. Over time, I matured a bit, not bawling my eyes out with tears whenever somebody had to leave. I realized it was a common thing in a foreign land for people to come and go. I was learning we are all sojourners and fellow travelers.

One big lesson I learned was to love and care for people because time is always short. While living in China, I knew when I met a friend, our time together might only be for a year or two. Whenever I returned to the Philippines, I knew my time with family and friends would be limited to a month or two, so I learned to make the most of my time there, too.

I also enjoyed the blessing of friendship with some single women who shared the same heart and emotional struggles. We met for coffee and meals, hiked together, shopped, rode bicycles, and did other fun activities. I realized and learned that friends are a gift from the Lord, and they are to be treasured. I learned the truth of the saying, "Friends and people come at different seasons for different reasons." I have learned, too, that God sends friends at specific times to be His hands and feet. As human beings, we tend to hang on to those friendships, but I am learning that the Lord sometimes sends friends and people our way to show His love and care at particular times. He has shown me not to hang on to people or friendships, but to see Him in each of those friendships. It took me a while to understand it is the love of the Lord in each of the persons that draws us together; He sends each person for a reason and a season. The Lord gives and the Lord takes away.

Unchanging Love

Unchanging love
You are my unchanging love
You pick me up when I am down
You cheer me up when I am sad
You give me love when I am feeling unworthy
You give me hope when there is no hope
You are my unchanging love
In my ups and downs
You are the constant One
You never change
Nothing moves you
Nothing takes you by surprise
You are always there by my side
When I need someone to care
You are my unchanging love

CHAPTER 13: HEROES OF FAITH AND THEIR CHALLENGES

But we have this treasure in earthen vessels, that the excellence of the power may be of God and not of us. We are hard-pressed on every side, yet not crushed; we are perplexed, but not in despair; persecuted, but not forsaken; struck down, but not destroyed – always carrying about in the body the dying of the Lord Jesus, that the life of Jesus also may be manifested in our body.
(2 Corinthians 4:7-10)

In Spring of 2001, I took a 36-hour train ride to another province in the central part of the country. I met with some local Christians in the area. We went to a restaurant and rented a room to have a meal and private conversations (for security reasons). Through translation, I was introduced to a group of men and women who were leading house church meetings. I do not remember much about the details of the meeting, but one thing I'll never forget was meeting a certain woman in the group. She was in her late 30s and did not speak English. Through a translator, I was told that she had just been released from jail for preaching the Gospel. Her face was radiantly beaming. With a big smile on her face, she said they were honored to suffer for Christ.

The church in the country has endured persecution for the past seventy years. In different periods, persecution and hostility against Christians came in different degrees and forms. Many Christians suffered violence during the years of communist reformation from around 1950 to the 1970s for not denying their faith. Others were forced to endure many years of work in labor camps.

From the 1980s to the 2000s, the forms and degree of persecution varied from region to region, between cities and rural areas. In some rural areas, Christians were beaten and put in jail, only being released after paying a fine. Then around 2010, I heard reports of Christians in some big cities suffering discrimination when their apartment leases or business permits were not renewed by landlords or property management agencies. Christian groups gathering in houses were constantly threatened. If they were not registered, they were called illegal. If they registered, then the church would be subject to government regulation and control. In recent international news (2015-2020), it has been reported that images of crosses on many church buildings have been taken down and that many homes have been forced to put up a poster of the new country leader, Chairman X.

When I first visited a city in the southwest in 1995, I heard of only a handful of local believers. When I moved there in 1997, I got to know more about the local church. I learned that in the big cities there were two kinds of churches. One was called the registered church and the other was called the house church. In the past, they called the registered church the Three-Self Patriotic Movement [xiv](TSPM).

The registered church was supposed to be recognized by the government, and usually they had a building/structure as a church. By contrast, the house church gathered in private houses or apartments. The registered church, according to some friends, was supposed to be regulated by a government office – similar to a department of religious affairs – with people and activities being monitored by government workers. In my first few years in the country, I did not have the opportunity to attend a registered church. However, during my last two years in the country (2011-2013), I had the opportunity to participate in a registered church in the northern part of the country.

Moreover, the people did not have easy access to outside (foreign) social media and other online Christian resources, but of course, some found ways to access them. Printed Christian teaching materials were rare, and Bible copies were limited. Whenever I traveled outside the country and came back, I brought in Christian books and CDs of praise songs in Mandarin. I realized how blessed we are in the free world to have easy access to Christian materials through television, radio, and online programs.

Most of my experience with the church in China, however, was with the house church, Consequently, I am sharing more about them. The house church usually gathered in small groups of ten to twenty believers in an apartment. Most of them met discreetly, not using musical instruments or sound systems to avoid attention from neighbors. Housing in that area was mostly in tenement buildings with seven floors. Each floor had two units.

Later, more tall buildings were built with up to twenty floors, housing four or more units per floor and having an elevator.

The Lord blessed me to meet several Christians who were associated with different house church groups. It was a privilege to get to know some of them and see the faithfulness of the Lord to the saints who were not just enduring but were victorious amid opposition, persecution, and trials. The church did not just suffer from pressures from the authorities, but some of them also suffered violence from cultic groups. Some were lured by false teachings. Many of the church leaders did not have theological or seminary training. They taught from the Bible with the very little knowledge and understanding they had. Two or three times every year, I heard of some small groups (house churches) in the city that were visited by policemen. When the news of policemen visiting a house church got around, many of them would stop meeting together. After some time, when things calmed down, the groups resumed their church meetings. This experience was from about twenty years ago; many changes have taken place in the house church situation since then. The degree of persecution in the southwest region during that period was not as intense as it was in some other regions like the central province. I think because there were fewer Christians, the Church was young in general and was not ready to take risks – to lose their jobs and their lives for something they knew little about – the Gospel and God. The church in other regions such as the central province had more exposure to the Gospel and had more strong disciples who were willing to risk everything for the sake of their Lord Jesus. However, in the past few years, as Christians grew in the southwest (in numbers and in faith), I heard more news of persecution. I was surprised to hear in the international news a couple of years ago (2019) of the arrest of some leaders of a church with about 500 members.

It was a privilege and a big blessing from the Lord for me to meet some of the local believers in the city who became brothers and sisters to me, mothers, and uncles. They were my heroes of faith. The Word of God says, ***"Remember the prisoners as if chained with them – those who are mistreated – since you yourselves are in the body also" (Hebrews 13:3).*** Here are some of their stories:

My friends and I met **Mrs. Zhen** in my second year in the city – around 1998. Mrs. Zhen was a retired medical doctor. In the Philippines, most medical doctors I knew were either in the middle or upper class. In that region, with a background of socialism, medical doctors, nurses, teachers, and government workers all had the same economic status. No one was considered rich or poor. So, Mrs. Zhen lived in the same tenement building as everyone else, except that she was on the top/seventh floor. Each time I visited her it was a sacrifice to climb the seven floors on foot to get to her apartment. When I got to the fifth floor, I usually paused to catch my breath. However, whenever I came, she prepared a good meal for me. My team and I also met her son and daughter, who were in their early 20s. Although neither of her children was a Christian at that time, Mrs. Zhen had become a believer through some of her older friends. She was eager to know God and the Bible. Her daughter, who became a good friend, accepted Jesus during a Christmas program my friends and I hosted.

I also found out Mrs. Zhen sometimes hosted a small group of other retired ladies and brothers in the Lord for Bible study. There were times she also attended other group gatherings. Though Mrs. Zhen loved the Lord and was very eager to know Him and His Words, she understood the risk of going to a church or a small group. She knew believers could be put in jail for attending Christian gatherings if not done in a designated or approved church building. For security and safety, they met on different days and not at the same time. She was happy when she found out she could also listen to Bible lessons on the radio, mostly through shortwave radio which was broadcast from other countries.

Mrs. Zhen had a rough life before becoming a Christian. Even though she did not say much about her past life, we knew that she had already been divorced from her husband for many years.

The first time my group met her in 1998, she and her group did not celebrate Christmas. With the few Chinese words that I knew at that time, I understood that they had been taught Christmas day is not the real birthday of Jesus. We did not discuss theology with her at that time because our Chinese language skills were inadequate. However, later on, we shared with her that many small groups in the city were using Christmas programs to evangelize their friends, neighbors, and colleagues. Later, when I visited her, she shared with me that her group had a Christmas program, and several had accepted Jesus as they heard the story of Christmas. I always enjoyed visiting with her as we shared a meal and prayed together.

In 2007 I moved back to the Philippines. However, when I again visited the city in 2013, the Lord blessed me to see Mrs. Zhen again. Both she and her daughter were thrilled to see me. She had prepared some of my favorite local dishes. She told me that she had just finished a Bible Course *through the shortwave radio*. Despite the challenges and risks of being a Christian and going to a local church, Mrs. Zhen had found a way to nurture her faith. The Lord satisfied her hunger for His Word through the radio ministry. (Later on, when I met my husband, I learned that he works for this same Christian radio ministry.) Her group still manages to meet whenever the situation in the city is conducive.

In my first year, through some friends, I met a church leader named **Brother Wang**. I did not know him well, but I heard he was passionate about sharing the Gospel. According to some friends, there was a time when this brother was caught distributing Christian materials in the city. He was jailed for a few days. Prior to his release, however, I heard news from friends that while he was in jail, he was able to witness, and even baptized some men in the jail!

The sad thing was when he got out of jail, I heard news through the grapevine that some local believers shunned him because they were afraid to be associated with him. Some of them had fears and speculations that anyone who was put in jail could be on the watchlist. Anyone seen meeting with that person might be associated with his religious activities and might be in trouble with the officials, too.

The Lord blessed me to know other local church workers in the southwest city. It was a privilege to be their friends and serve with them. One of them was **Brother Red.** He and his family came from the central province. Brother Red felt called to do ministry in our city, but he did not have higher education. He was a farmer in his province. When he and his family moved to that big city in the southwest, he struggled to make a living. He tried different odd jobs, but his heart was in ministry – to share Christ with others. A couple of years later, he managed to have a small group that met for Bible study. A few more workers came from his province to help him. Although Brother Red and his co-workers did not have formal Bible training, their small group of believers grew into several groups. Meanwhile Brother Red struggled to make a living to support his growing family in a big city.

Brother Red came to our training ministry. In addition to needing some practical help to support his family, he also needed Bible training to help his growing church. We encouraged him to teach his church about tithing and giving. Many times, Brother Red explained to us that he was reluctant to teach about money because some of the new believers came from a background of idol worship. He was concerned that they might think that tithing was the same as giving offerings to idols to appease the false gods. Brother Red did not want to discourage new believers from coming to church.

Our ministry group tried to help him financially. For a few years, he tried various small business ventures, but nothing worked out. It seems he did not have business and management skills. Besides, his background was in farming and his passion was evangelism. Once, he tried to drive a truck for rental but had a wreck because he did not really have driving skills. However, his church continued to grow, and he began to train new leaders to lead small groups.

Brother Red shared with us other challenges he experienced in doing ministry in the city. There were times when policemen came to his church meetings. With wisdom from the Lord, he managed to reason with the policemen. One time when some police came to his meeting and asked what they were doing as a group, he politely replied, "Well, we are studying this book called the Bible. We are not doing anything bad, not bothering anyone. See these are good people." With the Lord's grace, the police just left them alone.

I heard from other sources that people could gather in small groups if there were not more than fifteen to twenty people, and as long as they did not say or do anything against the government. However, some groups were afraid to gather because they thought it was illegal for them to do any kind of religious activities. They kept their groups very small and secret. Some of them were very careful about whom to invite, in fear of having a stranger who could be a government spy.

Another challenge facing the struggling local church was the threat from some cultic groups. I heard of two such groups: *Falun-gong and Eastern Lightning*. I did not know much about either of them since I had not personally met anyone from those groups. However, I heard some local church leaders speak about the dangers posed by those groups.

Brother Red shared with me that one of his church leaders had an encounter with one of the cultic groups in the city. According to Brother Red, one of his workers who lived in the countryside was kidnapped by some men from this cultic group. The church leader was beaten and threatened when he refused to join the group.

Other house churches also experienced members of cultic groups coming to church and claiming to be Christians. Then the cultic groups tried to convince the leaders of the church to join them. They argued that they were the right Christian group. If the leaders could not be persuaded, the members of the cultic group would take them by force and beat them.

Wolves in Sheep's clothing

One of the most heartbreaking experiences I had working with the house church was the story of Ling. For a few months, I worked in an international school in the city. I met Ling and her friend Dee while working in school. Ling and Dee were also friends with Natalie who worked in the other international school. They were a jolly bunch – Ling, Dee, and Natalie! They all had good English-speaking skills.

They were introduced to the Christian faith through another Christian worker while they were still in college. The three of them got involved with a local house church. A few times, the three of them came to our training program. They also helped us sometimes with translation work for the ministry. I noticed that Ling was the more serious type. She seemed to take her faith and learning the Bible very seriously. She had come to me a few times with several questions about the Bible. I enjoyed sharing with her during lunch hours or afternoon tea during weekends. Ling at times had led Bible lessons with her group. Compared to some other young people I knew, I was confident that Ling had a growing faith. She was eager to know more about the Christian faith.

A few months later, because of a visa issue, I had to leave my work in the school. I went back to the Philippines, and when I came back to the city a few months later, I heard disturbing news from Ling's friends. They said that Ling was missing. Her mother had asked them if they knew where she was. We waited for a few days for news to see if she would come back. None of her friends knew where she was. We prayed for her. Then a few days later, news came to me that Ling had run away. According to one of her friends, Ling had joined one of the cultic groups. We waited for days and months, but no news came about her. I am very sad to say I have not heard anymore since then. I still wonder about her even after many years. I hope and pray that the Lord has rescued her and gotten her back in the fold.

I also heard through some friends that another local church leader was lured by the Eastern Lighting group. I was not able to verify the news and did not have the opportunity to talk with him. Some other local Christians in the city had avoided being associated with him. It was a sad thing to hear such disturbing news. Part of the problem, I think, was that the local Christians often lacked good theological training and Bible teaching which caused some of them to be lured by cultic teachings. Part of the ministry I was involved in was training church leaders and workers. However, there were some challenges. Besides the language barrier, we were only able to invite those who were willing to come and risk being associated with foreign Christian activity.

A Church worker listening to a Christian program by shortwave radio

CHAPTER 14: VISIT TO A VILLAGE

"And we know that all things work together for good to those who love God, to those who are the called according to His purpose." (Romans 8:28)

January 2002

It was a winter evening when I met a local believer in a restaurant for dinner and a ministry meeting. We finished talking and paid the bill. My usual routine would be to visit the ladies' room. A few minutes later as I was about to leave the restaurant, I realized my purse was gone. It was a small purse made of colorful fabric with a black string as a handle that I usually hung like a sling on my body. I used that small purse to carry my passport and wallet whenever I went on out-of-town trips or international travel. I was planning to do an out-of-town trip the following day. So, when I realized I did not have my little purse, I ran to the ladies' room and found nothing. I asked the restaurant workers, and they said that nobody saw it. It had been only ten minutes since I had left the ladies room, but nobody had seen my purse! I did not remember seeing another customer coming in after me to the ladies' room. There were only a handful of guests in the restaurant that evening.

I had lost my purse! And my purse had my wallet, bank card, and the most important document a person living overseas has – a passport! I panicked and cried tears, but it did not help. With my bicycle, I managed to get home. On my way home, I stopped by the apartment of my team leader and broke the bad news. I praise the Lord for the kindness of this couple. They did not just sympathize with me, but they also gave me some money to help tide me over. The Lord also gave me wisdom to call my home church in the Philippines to cancel my bank card. I thank the Lord for the help of our church accountant.

Meanwhile, as I mentioned, I had planned to do an out-of-town trip the following day with some other local believers. We were going to a mountain city to do outreach to an ethnic group in the northwest part of the province. After spending 8 to 10 hours on a bus, we finally arrived and went to our hotel. Normally, to register for a hotel room, I would have had to give them a copy of my passport. But, since I was sharing a room with one of the girls on our team, we used her local ID (identification card) to register. I think it also helped that I was Asian; the hotel staff may not have noticed that I was a foreigner. I did not mean to mislead. I prayed about the situation, and the Lord intervened. Although I was discouraged about the loss of the passport and had a heavy heart, the Lord sustained and kept me during my time in the mountain city. With the Lord's grace, our team was still able to minister to the local people in the village.

After returning from our trip, I filed a police report, hoping my passport would at least be returned. But nothing came back to me. For a few weeks, I was uncomfortable and nervous being without a passport, but I thanked the Lord that I still had a residence permit. It is hard to describe how disconcerting and nerve-racking it was to be going around in a foreign land without a passport.

For many days, I did not have a passport, and did not know what to do. I could apply for a new passport at the Philippine Embassy, which was in the capital city of the country in the northeast, about a three-hour flight away or 36 hours by train. But I did not have access to the funds, because my bank card was gone, too. Even if I had the funds, I did not have the passport to buy a plane ticket. "Oh Lord, what do I do?" was my prayer and dilemma.

Finally, after about a month, the Lord sent me help. My home church in the Philippines sent me extra funds to get a new passport. Since I had no passport to buy a plane ticket, I took the long-distance train, a trip which took about 36 hours as mentioned earlier. The Lord also provided a good place for me to stay. A Filipino friend, who was a teacher in the capital city, invited me to stay in her apartment. That was a big help so that I did not have to spend money for a hotel room. The Lord gave me favor and helped me complete the paperwork to get a new passport. I stayed a few days with my friend and was able to do some sightseeing and take a little tour while I was waiting for the release of my passport. Once again, the Lord's kindness was shown through sisters and brothers in the Lord who helped me with practical needs. The trip to the big city provided a few days of rest and retreat from ministry work, and some much-needed relief from all the emotional stress due to the loss of my passport and bank card.

Prior to my trip to the north, Brother Red, one of the local church leaders in the southwest, had invited me to visit his hometown in the central region of the country. When he found out I was traveling to the north, he suggested that I visit his village during the same trip. He told me that his home church had a yearly gathering of house church leaders and workers. This gathering would take place at about the same time that I would be finished with my passport process in the north. If I took the long-distance train, the central province was exactly mid-point between my travel from the north to the south.

In my mind, I imagined a workers' conference like the pastors' conferences we usually had in my home country, held in nice church buildings or rented auditoriums with elaborate programs. I left for my trip and told Brother Red, "I will try to come," but made no promise. Another church co-worker, a common friend of Brother Red and mine, told me that he and a couple of local church workers were planning to go with Brother Red. With the knowledge that other people I knew were going, I felt comfortable to go, but was not sure how it would work out.

Back to the city in the north, the Lord gave me success and favor with the staff of the Philippine Embassy. I got a new passport, praise the Lord! I made plans to return to the southwest city, again, via train ride. I prayed and felt led to consider the invitation of Brother Red. I had often heard stories of followers of Christ in that central region. According to some reports, that region was known for its large and growing number of believers. However, the place was also known for its persecution of believers. So, I thought it would be a privilege and honor to visit believers in that region.

I took the long-distance train from the north to the central province. I enjoyed the 12-hour train ride during which I saw a nice view of the countryside from the train window. Almost every hour, the train stopped at a major city. Many people on the train went down to buy food from small peddlers who came to the train platform. I also enjoyed a little walk on the train platform for just three or four minutes. After 12 hours, the train arrived at our destination. Sure enough, it was an adventure of faith, and became one of the highlights of my entire mission experience!

I received instructions from Brother Red via telephone on how to get a bus from the train station to the city. After about a two-hour bus ride, I arrived in a small city. Brother Red, accompanied by a couple of other men, met me at the bus station. I thought we had arrived, but it was not the end of the long journey yet. The men took me to a small car, and then we drove on a dirt road past many farming fields to a small village. It was the middle of winter, so all the surrounding area was brown and dry. I heard that they were having a drought.

The men brought me to one of the farmhouses, and a family hosted me. We ate supper with some of the church leaders. Together with my host and the church leaders, we had a good sharing time. I asked them about persecution of believers that

I had heard about in their region. One of the brothers answered my question and then commented by saying something like, "Being in jail for us is as normal as eating a meal." He said it very casually, and the others laughed along with him. Another brother said that his sister was actually in jail at that very time. The brother added that, in the past, they had paid monetary fines to be released. Then they realized they were being extorted for money, so they stopped paying fines. He then continued to say that his sister was still in jail, and that some of them used such instances as an opportunity to share the Gospel with others who were in jail.

Early the next morning, around 4:00 to 5:00 a.m., I was awakened by some sounds. I heard some people walking and talking softly outside the house. I found out later that the people I heard were other believers coming to the meeting place. I was told that I didn't have to get ready until 8:00 a.m. Someone told me that some church workers from the area had wanted to get to the meeting place early. They also tried to be discreet by coming one at a time so that they did not attract too much attention from other neighbors. After breakfast, a couple of sisters brought me to the meeting place which was about a ten-minute walk through the wheat fields. When I got there, they had already finished their singing and worship time. The meeting and study lasted all day for a few days. To my surprise, the place was a small barn turned into a worship meeting place. They put some wooden benches and an old wooden pulpit in the place which was full of people: men and women, young and old. Some were sitting on the dirt floor and some were sitting on stacks of hay at the back. Maybe around 80 to 100 people were huddled together on a cold winter's day. The barn was made of mud brick which they used to store their crops. Many of the church workers were farmers, herders, or taxi and pedicab drivers. I saw many faces I did not know, but there were three men I recognized. They were the church co-workers and friends from the same city in the southwest I have mentioned earlier. With Brother Red, they had arrived a day earlier and were staying in another house. I found out later that many of those who came to the meeting were church leaders and workers from around the village and other nearby villages. Most of them rode their bikes or walked on foot for 10 or 20 miles. Some lived nearer and some farther, but a lot of them came early. They all looked radiant with beaming faces. I did not understand much of the speaking and sharing in their dialect, but I could see in their faces the joy, excitement, and hunger for the Word of God.

Another big surprise for me was when I was asked to teach and share words with the group for their workers' conference. I should not have been surprised, I suppose, since they usually do that. Whenever I visited a local church, I was asked to say some words of greeting or a word of encouragement. But I forgot that aspect and had not prepared to teach. I did not bring a Bible lesson with me since I only came to visit and to have fellowship. Well, anyway, with the help of the Holy Spirit, I managed to share some words of encouragement from the Bible one morning.

Someone whispered to me that a year before, some police had come to the same kind of gathering and some church leaders had been put in jail. Then he pointed out to me a brother standing in a corner as being one of those who had been jailed the previous year. I told myself, "Great, that's not encouraging. Why are they having the same meeting in the same place if some of them were jailed already! Where is wisdom here?" So, I prayed a lot for the Lord's protection for the entire few days I was there. My concern was not just for myself but also for them since I was a foreigner. I had heard that they could be in trouble if a foreigner were with them at a local church gathering. I had heard stories of foreigners who were asked to leave the country because they were found practicing religion with the locals. Well, again, I prayed a lot and trusted the Lord for His protection.

At noontime, we stopped for a lunch break. I saw that some women were busy at the back of the barn preparing a meal. They used a stove made of three big stones and a fire started from a few sticks of wood to cook. They had a big pot of vegetables and a lot of steamed buns *(baozi)*. Many helped in the kitchen, and we all ate together.

The meetings and Bible teachings went on for the next few days from morning to evening. For the next two to three nights, I stayed in different homes. I was not sure if they wanted to protect me as a foreigner or if different homes wanted to host me. I just did what I was told. Each family was kind and hospitable. The biggest challenge I had was concerning personal needs. I noticed the houses I stayed in did not have proper indoor plumbing or a bathroom. So, one time I went out and found that the *potty place* was a hole in the ground next to the pig pen. I tried my best to stay far from the pigs, who were trying to smell me :). One night, I went outside and tried to look for a spot behind a tree or something, but to my dismay, the outside was all flat farm fields, and since it was a dry winter, nothing was growing. There was no spot to do my business discreetly. Since it was winter, I managed with a lot of prayer and grace not to have a shower for about seven days. But the biggest challenge to my health was not finding a suitable place to relieve my tummy.

After three days of church meetings, I asked some of the brothers to help me find a train ticket and told them that I needed to get back to my home in the southwest. I was told it was not easy to get a train ticket at that time. I thought they were trying to get me to stay for another week at the workers' conference. But with all the inconveniences of staying in farmhouses, with no facility available to clean myself, I struggled with my attitude. (Later, I had to ask the Lord for forgiveness. Being young and immature, I did not handle the situation well.) I was also concerned about joining the big church workers' meeting as a foreigner. After four days, they managed to find me a train ticket to return to my home in the southwest! A couple of men took me to the train station. Oh, I was so relieved when I got home to my apartment after a 24-hour train ride and being away for two weeks! I was thankful to be home, to have a shower, and to have clean clothes after seven days. It felt good, too, to have my stomach relieved. I was amazed how the Lord protected me during the trip, taking care of my health. I was also thankful that no police came to the meeting, and nobody got put in jail. Still, I am grateful to the Lord for that experience.

Reflection

Looking back, I was truly honored to meet the brothers and sisters in the Lord in that region of the country. Their faith has been well spoken of in the Body of Christ, not just in that country, but also in other countries. It was a privilege for me to meet them and see their actual conditions. Many of them may have appeared poor in the physical realm, but they were rich in the Spirit. They had endured many hardships, persecutions, and trials for their faith, yet they remained steadfast in their love for the Lord. I heard from one of them that they felt honored to be persecuted and suffer for Christ. They took the words of Jesus seriously in Matthew 5:11-12: "Blessed are you when they revile and persecute you...Rejoice and be exceedingly glad, for great is your reward in heaven..."

Concerning my personal situation, I also thanked the Lord for His faithfulness as I went through the challenge of losing my purse and passport. The words of the Apostle Paul in the Bible proved true in that situation: *"And we know that all things work together for good to those who love God, to those who are the called according to His purpose." (Romans 8:28)*

The Lord worked something good out of a very unpleasant experience. Even with the loss of my purse and passport, a very good thing came out of the situation. I was able to make a trip to that other region and had an amazing experience of meeting some heroes of the faith.

JESUS YOU GAVE YOUR ALL

Jesus You gave your all
Jesus You gave all of yourself
For a sinner like me
You gave your all
Words are not enough to say
Thank you my Lord
How could you love a sinner like me?
You gave your whole self to us all
With your nails-pierced hands
Bruised, wounded and all,
All because of love for us all
Jesus Your deep love
Nothing and no one could ever compare
For the love You have shown
Jesus You gave Your all
Body, soul, and all
This is the greatest love of all

CHAPTER 15: THE YOUNG PEOPLE AND THEIR CHALLENGES

*"Delight yourself also in the LORD,
And He shall give you the desires of your heart."
(Psalm 37: 4)*

Merriam, a young single woman in the southwest city, shared with me one time, "Vicki, in my church group, we are all single women. Even our church leader is single and still waiting. In my mother's church, there are mostly older people. Where are the single Christian men?"

Like other Christian young women in the city, Merriam had asked me the same questions about why there were not many available single Christian men. Like young people in other parts of the world, they had other issues and questions.

The Lord blessed me to meet some fine young people like Merriam during my time in the southwest city. Some of them were college students and young professionals. Many of them were eager to learn about the outside world and especially the English language. For some of them, learning another language was key to getting good jobs with foreign companies, and higher education was very important to them. A lot of them also came from one-child families. In general, many children born under the one-child policy (see note xi) were known to be pampered. Most of them had at least six adults who cared a lot for them – parents and two sets of grandparents. Some of them could be used to having their own way or getting what they wanted. However, I was blessed that most of the young people I met were kind, thoughtful, and loyal friends.

For a lot of them, Christianity was not part of their culture nor their education. Their families or parents were either non-religious or followers of traditional idol worshipping religions. The handful of Christians they knew were mostly foreigners. In the late 1990s and early 2000s internet access and social media were not available. (Currently, social media from outside the country is still not accessible to the public). So, most of them did not have much Christian influence in their lives. A lot of them had not heard the Gospel nor had they heard of the name of Jesus. They thought of Christianity as a western religion. Some of them were familiar with Christmas, but they thought it was about Santa Claus. For those who did not have any concept of Christianity or exposure to the Gospel, it took them a long time to believe. Their faith journey was a little bit different from most of us who have a Judeo-Christian background.

Coming from a Judeo-Christian background, we have usually heard evangelistic messages such as, "God loves you and has a wonderful plan for your life." Most of us are familiar with John 3:16, "For God so loved the world that He gave His only begotten Son, that whoever believes in Him should not perish but have everlasting life." In sharing the Gospel with the people in that culture, I learned that to tell someone that God loves them is a totally foreign concept. First, they were taught that there is no God and religion is not good. To believe in the God of heaven is a giant step for them. The first big hurdle is to help them believe that God in heaven exists, since evolution is a big part of their educational training.

Those who believed usually kept it to themselves fearing the risk of being ostracized by their families, friends, or colleagues at work. Those who worked in the government could lose their jobs. One of my friends who decided to be a Christian after hearing the Gospel for almost ten years kept her faith from her parents and colleagues for a long time.

I often enjoyed sharing meals with believers over Chinese noodles, dumplings, or other spicy dishes. One of the favorite meals to share with families and friends is a dish called *huoguo*. It is one of the most famous dishes in the cuisine of the southwest with a literal meaning of "hot pot," a hot and spicy dish which is mostly served in restaurants and in street markets. During summer, many streets in the city have rows of small wooden tables and chairs. In the middle of the tables, there is a metal cooking pot sitting on a small stove which is fueled from underneath. The pot has a broth of spicy hot peppers and other spices. When the broth gets boiling, they put vegetables, meat, and other raw ingredients into it. When the food is cooked, they dip them in a spicy sauce. Even though spicy food was not my favorite, I enjoyed chit-chat and ministry meetings over *hot pot* meals with some of the young people.

Some of them were adventurous to try western meals. Whenever I had time to prepare and cook a meal, I invited them to my apartment. Christian holidays like Easter and Christmas were good opportunities to invite them to my apartment and introduce them to faith. There were times also when they invited me to their homes where I enjoyed authentic local dishes and home-cooked meals. One of my favorites was making Chinese dumplings. I enjoyed visiting and sharing meals with their families during Chinese New Year, a holiday in early spring, usually in February. They also invited me during their birthdays. I was a bit surprised that some of them celebrated their birthdays on different days each year, using a lunar calendar. However, some of them celebrated their birthdays using the Roman calendar which, of course, is a fixed date every year.

Some of the young people I met were young believers. Through sharing meals, tea, or coffee, I got to know them better as I listened to their personal stories. I learned of their struggles in dealing with parents, their jobs, faith, and other issues in life. The following are some of their stories.

Merriam

One Christmas, my friend Li and I hosted a celebration, and Merriam came. It was her first time to celebrate Christmas and to hear the true story of the holiday. Praise the Lord, Merriam opened her heart to Jesus! After that, we became good friends and had some Bible studies with her. She had many questions about life. In the past, she thought the

Christian religion was only for older people because she saw that her mother's Bible Study group was mostly made up of the elderly. When she met our group and met other young people, she felt encouraged and started coming to our small group. Merriam was curious to know God, but I observed turmoil in her heart. Just like any other young person, she wrestled with making Christianity relevant to her life. She liked beauty, fashion, arts, fun, and *the good life* just like other young people.

Merriam had many talents and had often changed jobs. She also started her own business, selling clothes that she designed. There was a time when she even moved to a bigger city to find a better job with a cosmetic company. I knew her mother was concerned about her. We thanked the Lord that after a few months she moved back to her home city.

One time, Merriam invited Li and me for lunch at a restaurant. Afterward, we went to her apartment. She opened up to me and to Li how she struggled with doubts about her faith in God. At that time, we had already spent almost a year studying the Bible with her. While talking with her, we saw in her apartment books on worshipping traditional idols. She shared with us that those books belonged to her stepmother. She had read those books because she was seeking and trying to understand God and religion. We felt led to pray with her for deliverance from the lies of false gods and to be cut off from the influence of idols. We then encouraged her to read the Bible. Since that time, she started to grow in her faith. She still had some questions about the Bible and was still trying to understand the One True God, but we saw that she started to grow, slowly but surely.

After a couple of years, Merriam got to know a small group of young ladies who met for Bible Study and fellowship. As she got to know more Christians in the city, her faith grew. She even started to serve in her small group. Her small group leader was also a good friend of mine, and I was happy to hear from her about Merriam's growth. Later, as the years went by, I continued to meet Merriam whenever I visited her mom, Mrs. Zhen. Her mom was also happy to see her daughter grow in her relationship with the Lord.

However, like other young women, as I mentioned in the opening, Merriam also had emotional struggles with being single and waiting for God's will regarding marriage. I assumed her mother, who loves God and the Word of God, had encouraged her to wait for a Christian man. I also assumed that Merriam might have been familiar with the words in the Bible, *"Do not be unequally yoked together with unbelievers. For what fellowship has righteousness with lawlessness? And what communion has light with darkness? (2 Corinthians 6:14)*

When she asked why it seemed there were not many Christian single men available, and the Christian men she knew were mostly older like her mom's friends, I understood her struggle because she was already in her late twenties and still single. Being single myself, all I could say in sympathy to her was something like, "I understand, and it is not easy to wait on the Lord's will. But He will give us the grace. I am also praying and waiting like you."

One time, I found a good Christian book on dating which was translated into Chinese. I shared it with Merriam who was excited to read it. After some months, I asked her if she could return the book so I could share it with other sisters in the Lord. To my surprise, she told me that she had already passed the book on to other single ladies in her group. She did not know where the book was since it had been passed on to others. I was glad that the book helped some of those young women to know more about dating the Christian way.

Looking back, I am thankful to the Lord for my years of waiting for marriage which helped me understand more about the emotional struggles of other young people. Even though I myself struggled to have patience in waiting for the Lord, many times I tried to encourage those young ladies from the Word of the Lord: *"Delight yourself also in the LORD, And He shall give you the desires of your heart...Rest in the LORD, and wait patiently for Him..." (Psalm 37:4, 7)*

The last time I saw Merriam was in 2013. I had not seen her for a few years, so we were very glad to get together again. She was still single and waiting. However, I saw a glimmer of hope in her eyes. She was excited to share with me the good news that her church leader was engaged to be married to another church leader. She looked happy for her church leader, and at the same time, hopeful as she witnessed how God answers prayer. It is my prayer that the

Lord will bring a godly man to Merriam, in case she is not married yet.

Joli

I met Joli while working at the International School. She was sweet, kind, and always helpful. She became a believer through the influence of other Christians in the city, both local and foreign. Like many other young believers, she too had struggled with her faith in God. But I saw her persevere, and she was always eager to learn. She had a servant's heart and enjoyed serving and helping others. Joli was already in her mid-twenties. Her parents were not Christians yet, and she was the only child in the family. Her parents had bought an apartment unit for her so she could be prepared for her own family. Joli was starting to learn and understand the Bible. She knew the Bible says not to marry unbelievers. However, she felt pressure from her parents who were anxious for her to find a man so that they could have grandchildren. I knew this issue was a big challenge for Joli. Some of our friends had persistently encouraged her to wait for the Lord, and she had waited for some years. However, in 2014, after more than ten years of waiting, I heard news from a common friend that Joli got married! According to our common friend, she was not sure if the man was a Christian, but he was a colleague in her work. Joli had waited many years for a Christian man to come, but sad to say, it did not happen. So, Joli, who was in her late 30s, finally married someone. I heard they had their first child in 2015.

Natalie

Natalie also worked in an international school. She was cute and wore a smile all the time. She was introduced to Christianity through a foreign teacher at her college. The seed the Lord planted through that teacher was watered through other Christians who came to the International School. I had the privilege of seeing Natalie grow in her child-like faith. A couple of years later, she became involved with a local church group. I was happy to see her grow in her walk with the Lord as she served in her church. Natalie was the only child of her parents who lived in another province. They belonged to an ethnic group, but she was diligent about getting an education and worked hard in her job. She and other Chinese girls sometimes came to my apartment where we "hung out" together. I was intentional about sharing my faith with the young women. We did not have formal Bible studies since I knew they already had a small group or local church, but I was determined to have a positive influence on them through our friendship. I wanted those young ladies to know God in a more personal way and to make Christianity relevant in their lives. I had learned through some leadership training courses that one meaning of leadership is *influence*.

In Chinese culture, relationship and trust are important. So, for these young women to trust someone, they needed to feel comfortable and safe. I felt good that they felt safe enough to trust me even though I was a foreigner. Through our friendships, they were able to share with me personal situations.

As a result, I was able to share with them from the Word of God and how to apply it in their life situations. I thank the Lord that through His Spirit in me those young women felt comfortable.

One of those young women who seemed comfortable with me was Natalie. As I mentioned earlier, she and some of the other young women would sometimes come to my apartment. We had meals together, had times of sharing, and watched movies on DVD.

On some weekends, the young women spent the night in my apartment. Even though my apartment was small, we all squeezed in and had fun watching movies together. I enjoyed spending time with them, individually or as a group over Chinese meals. Sometimes, they had questions about the Bible or their faith. I was glad to share with them and explain to them what I knew or understood.

One time, Natalie came to visit by herself. After sharing a meal, we watched a movie on my DVD player. The movie was about God, but not really a Christian film. After watching the movie, Natalie shared with me that she was reminded to be serious about her relationship with God. I was a bit surprised since the movie was not a Christian movie, it was just a Hollywood movie about God. However, I then realized that God can communicate with us all in different ways to connect at our present level, as He had done with Natalie.

After a few years, I moved back to the Philippines and served in other places. When I visited the southwest city in 2013, the Lord blessed me to visit some old friends. I was happy to see Natalie again. She was still a faithful believer and was still going to a local church or small group. She was still working at the International School. It was a delight to see her. She shared with me the good news that she was in a serious relationship. She was waiting for a visa from the U.S. Consulate to be with her fiancé in the United States so they could prepare for their wedding.

In 2015, I heard news that she got married and moved here to the United States. In 2016, the Lord blessed me to travel to the northeastern part of the United States where I got to visit Natalie and her new family. I was happy to see how the Lord blessed her and her faithfulness with a loving husband and cute little son.

Grace and Brother Haylee

The story of Grace and her husband, Brother Haylee, is one of my favorite stories among the young people. My friend Li and I met Grace during our second year of Chinese study through another friend. In her early 20s, Grace was a sweet young lady and was always full of joy. She was one of the workers in her small church group in the northern part of the city. Whenever we had time to meet with her, we took time to encourage one another in the Word and pray for each other.

One day she came and visited us in our apartment at the university. She looked unusually bewildered. We knew her to have a candid and bubbly personality. The day she came to our place, she did not look like herself. So, we asked her, "How are you? What is going on?"

She replied with a soft and gentle answer in English, "Well, there is a brother in our church...ah, I am a bit bothered."

She told us about a brother who had been coming to their church fellowship. Although she knew him, they had never actually spoken. Then one day, the brother surprisingly talked with her about being his wife. Li and I were both shocked.

A month later we met Grace again and were surprised to learn that she and the brother were planning to get married. Grace, with giggles and a laugh, replied to us, "We spoke with some elders in our church about our situation, and they all think it is the will of God for us to get married. I prayed about it, and I also feel it is the will of God. I want to be obedient to the Lord."

It did not take very long. Grace and Brother Haylee got married after a month. They did not need a lot of preparation. They got a wedding license from their local government wedding registry and had a simple wedding in their small house church. Most couples I knew usually went through the stages of friendship, courtship, relationship, and engagement for many months or at least a year before they got married. However, with Grace and Brother Haylee, it was a different story. They were both mature in age and in the faith. They both thought, "If it is the Lord's will, then we just have to obey."

Both Grace and Brother Haylee came from simple families with low incomes. They did not have much. Grace worked in a small government office, while Brother Haylee was a full-time church worker. He was actually an evangelist who went to the countryside to share the Gospel and do Bible teaching. It was a joy to meet Brother Haylee. Grace and Brother Haylee shared a common love for the Lord and a passion to share the Gospel with others. Together, they were a good couple and could enjoy serving the Lord together.

A year later, I came back to the city after a furlough in the Philippines. One day, I took time to visit Grace and Brother Haylee. Grace had just delivered a healthy baby boy. Brother Haylee was a happy husband and proud new father. He continued to serve the Lord by traveling to the countryside with his team, preaching and sharing the Gospel in a discreet way. He also participated in some of the ministry training events of which I was a part. Through the years, whenever we had time, we enjoyed visiting each other.

When I visited the city in 2013, I was thrilled to see the family again. By that time, their son was already a young man studying in middle school. I was happy to know that Grace and Brother Haylee were faithfully serving the Lord in their local house church.

I also got to know other small groups of young believers in the city. One time, a few of us were led to organize a badminton game at a nearby sports complex for some young men and women from different church groups. In addition to getting some good exercise, we all enjoyed the fellowship and opportunity to make new friendships. Through that sports fellowship, some friendships started to grow among us, not necessarily romantic relationships, but some opportunities for networking and cooperative ministry efforts. If nothing else, many of the young believers were encouraged to know they were not alone in their faith. Small group leaders began to be friends with other small group leaders. They had joint Christmas programs and occasional joint Bible Studies. In the past, I had heard of some issues with mistrust among the different groups, so it was a blessing to see that Christians from different groups began to be more open to cooperation and fellowship. Later, some of them were encouraged to join small mission trips outside the city to reach ethnic groups with the love of Christ. One of my highest joys during my time of ministry in the southwest city was to see some of the young believers join local mission trips and reach out to the ethnic minorities in the region.

Hot pot, a famous meal in the southwest I enjoyed with friends

CHAPTER 16: FRIENDS IN THE MOUNTAIN CITY

My sheep wandered through all the mountains, and on every high hill; yes, My flock was scattered over the whole face of the earth, and no one was seeking or searching for them.
(Ezekiel 34:6)

It was a beautiful autumn day in October 2003 in a small mountain village in the northern part of the province. The people in that region are an ethnic group called J'rong. They speak a different language from the main language of Mandarin, and they have a different culture. The main religion is worshipping traditional idols.

I was with a small group of young Christians from the southwest city. We were visiting the village to share the love of God by giving some candies and small toys to the children. After more than an hour of playing with the children, I took time to rest and sit on a big rock by the side of the dirt road. The sky looked beautiful in blue and white. The sun was shining bright, but I still felt the coolness of the air. I could see some tall mountains from afar, and further down the valley was a cornfield ready for harvest. I was enjoying the picturesque scenery, a big contrast to the gray, gloomy, and dusty city where I lived. However, thoughts were interrupted when a young girl came to sit next to me. I snapped out of my reverie and quickly expressed my gratitude to her. "MJ, thank you so much for helping us," I said. "You are such a big help. It seems the children enjoyed the candies and toys." MJ, with a big smile on her face replied, "I am happy to help. I feel very happy whenever you all come to visit us."

I was looking at the rest of the team of young people who were still playing with the children. As I returned to look at MJ, I saw her countenance change to a curious look. Then she asked, "*Jiejie* (big sister), I noticed there were some colorful bracelets in the packages you gave to the children. What are those?" I pulled one from my backpack and showed it to her. "You mean this bracelet with colorful beads?" "Yes, what are those?" She looked at it with her eyes full of curiosity. I forgot that in their religion, they use prayer beads to pray to their idols, except their chain of beads is plain brown. I was a bit taken aback and was not really prepared for her question. "Well, actually each colorful bracelet bead has a story with it. Each color represents something," I managed to say in Chinese. MJ was very attentive and listened carefully. I thank the Lord that although I had only simple words in my Mandarin Chinese Christian vocabulary, my simple words actually helped MJ to understand because Mandarin was her second language. Her first language was J'rong. I proceeded to explain the beads to her in my simple way. "Yellow represents the color of heaven. Black is the color of the sinful heart of man. Red is the color of the blood of Jesus. When we believe Jesus, our hearts become clean, like the white bead. Green is the color of new life in Jesus Christ." With a puzzled look on her face, MJ asked curiously, "Who is Jesus?"

The story of MJ began a year and a half earlier when a small team of Americans who were missionaries in the Philippines had come to visit me in the southwest city: Keith, Cy, David, and Kat. The team leader, Keith, happened to know a common friend, Daniel, who was also serving as a short-term missionary in the same area where I was. I was always grateful to the Lord whenever a group of friends came to visit me in China. Our city in the southwest was not easily accessible from the outside world. There were no direct flights from the Philippines nor from other countries to that city. It was, therefore, a joy whenever there were friends or teams coming from the Philippines or the USA.

My friendship with MJ begins in the context of such a visit. It was May 2002, springtime in the southwest. The small team of Americans made plans to visit an ethnic people group with whom Daniel had been doing some research work. It was an 8 to 10-hour bus ride from the southwest city, along a rugged mountain road, at an elevation of 4,000 to 8,000 feet above sea level. The road trip reminded me of my very first trip in 1995 to another mountain city in the same plateau region. The mountains were huge, lush, and green. I noticed some altars associated with their traditional religion along the road and some colorful paper prayer flags hanging on lines that dotted the big, tall, green mountain. The local people believed that the prayers written on those colorful papers could reach their gods. A wild river ran along the sides of the mountain road, and a steep ravine plunged on the other side of the road.

After almost five hours of travel, our bus driver stopped for a lunch break by the roadside in a small town. At last, we could stretch our legs after a long time of sitting on the bus. The little restaurant was a 'hole in the wall' with a dirt floor and some small, bare, wooden tables with wooden stools. All the passengers in the bus – about 80 people – hurriedly came down from the bus and filled the small restaurant. We enjoyed steamy rice, vegetables, and noodles. After the lunch break, our bus continued to travel, and I noticed the road got higher and higher in elevation.

After another four hours, our bus arrived at our destination – a beautiful and quaint city nestled between two big mountains with a river running through it. I noticed the local ethnic people did not look like the people from the mainland. They wore traditional clothing of black or dark green woolen robes. The men had cowboy-looking hats and a knife or dagger tucked into their waistbands. The women wore nice colorful headgear with a piece of black fabric over their long, braided hair. A lot of the young people, however, dressed like the young people in the big city, wearing blue jeans and jackets. Because the weather was cooler, many were wearing jackets and coats. After we checked into the hotel – there was only one hotel that allowed foreigners – we walked into town. We found a small restaurant and had supper. It was a very long day for most of us after the 10-hour bus ride over those rugged mountain roads.

Visit to a temple

The following morning after breakfast, Daniel, who knew the town well, called a local taxi to take us to the next town. We then hiked a few miles through the hills and finally reached a monastery and temple nestled on top of a hill.

In the courtyard of the temple building, we saw several older men and women sitting on the steps at the side of the entrance to the monastery. They were wearing their traditional clothes – black woolen robes over layers of clothing to shield them from the cold weather. I saw that their clothing looked worn out with colors faded from many years of exposure to the sun in cold winters. The women were wearing aprons, tied around their waists, over their woolen robes. In their culture, women wear aprons to symbolize that they are married. They also wore black headgear over their braided gray hair that was coiled on top of their heads. The two old men wore traditional clothing of woolen robes over their trousers. They wore shirts with colorful stripes on the edges and old leather cowboy hats. Wrinkle lines on their faces reflected years of hardships. Each man had a chain of beads in one hand and a prayer wheel in the other hand as they chanted prayers to their gods in their local dialect. When they saw us, they stopped their prayers and greeted us with big smiles. Our guide, Daniel, introduced the four white-looking strangers to them. Even though we did not understand each other's languages, we were able to communicate with signs and handshakes. These

J'rong people were, of course, speaking their ethnic language which I had never heard before.

We stepped further inside the entrance of the main monastery building which was made of hardwood walls with a cement floor. We saw two older women walking around a big round wooden structure that turned around as the women moved. It was a big prayer wheel. They were holding prayer beads and chanting.

We walked further inside the entrance of the monastery building. It looked dark inside, and I noticed some colorful paintings and posters of grotesque-looking images of their idols hanging on the wall.

A young man, wearing a long red and yellow robe, came out to greet us. He was in his early to mid-twenties. The young monk looked happy when he recognized our team guide, Daniel. They seemed to know each other well. Prior to our trip, Daniel had already made several trips to this mountainous city and had made good friends among the local people. Daniel introduced our team. The young monk spoke some English and Mandarin, so I was able to communicate with him. He told us that the old men and women had come there almost every day for many years to pray. The young monk invited us to go inside the temple. We saw colorful paintings and images. He explained how the images and paintings related to their traditional beliefs, which I would call worship of idols and false gods. Basically, their religion was based on doing good and following their creeds. If they lived a good life, their next life would be good, but if they lived a bad life, their next life would be bad. Basically, they believed in reincarnation, a belief about coming back to life either as animals, insects, or another person. If they do very well in their next life, they might become one of their gods. The highest goal in their lifetime, therefore, is to be good, to make many prayers – like what the older people were doing – and eventually to become another god.

I learned that in their culture and religion, young men who became monks are taught by older men called *lamas* or teachers. The *lamas* teach the young monks to read their scriptures and meditate. The monks are usually brought there as young boys, around nine to twelve years old. Usually, the local people believe that a boy in the family should serve their gods as early as possible. Their religious 'scriptures' are books in their own language, that for the most part only religious leaders can read. Since the whole country is ruled by Han Chinese, all education is taught in the official Chinese language, Mandarin. However, the ethnic religious leaders are able to preserve their own written script through their studies in the religious temples and monasteries.

We were ushered into the main hall of the monastery where I saw large images of different idols in bronze and silver. There were several baskets of fruit, flowers, and some coins and paper bills of money lying on the altar. After showing us the different statues and images of their idols, the young monk led us to the back room which looked dark. We followed him as he climbed a narrow wooden ladder. I was afraid to miss a step, so I climbed the ladder carefully. The rest of the team followed. The young man offered us a seat in the main living room of the monastery. It was like a private room for the monks and their guests. The room looked colorful with posters of different images of idols. I noticed the traditional furniture – center tables and cabinets which were made of wood painted with red and orange flowers and green leaves with turquoise blue edging. We were offered a seat on a long wooden bench which had a traditional colorful futon mattress on it. From there he brought us to the deck of the monastery. It was a nice courtyard on the second floor of the building which faced the nearby beautiful mountains. It was nice to be outside of the dark and oppressive interior of the monastery building. We all enjoyed the feel of the warm sunshine on our skin and the gentle breezes of the cool air. We had a good visit. Both the young monk and the older people made us feel welcome.

Paul's home

The next day we visited a local home. Most of the houses outside the town were traditional structures made of fieldstone put together with cement and mud. Compared to the apartments and tall buildings of the big cities, the houses in J'rong Land were individually built. The next neighbor might be miles away. A traditional J'rong house was usually only two to three stories tall. The first story was usually open with a dirt floor where they kept their animals and harvest of barley or vegetables. We saw some animals in the field which looked a bit like cows. I found out they were called *yaks;* they looked like cows but were bigger and hairier. They also had goats, sheep, and some chickens.

We climbed a narrow stairway that led to the main living room. There Daniel introduced us to our host, a young man named Paul, a high school student at the local school. Paul also spoke some English. He called his mother from the kitchen and introduced us. He mentioned that his father was working in the field. Their simple house had colorful designs of flowers and trees on the walls. Paul had a poster of his favorite singing group pasted on the wall. I saw a colorful wooden tray on the coffee table in the middle of the living room containing different assortments of candies and some walnuts. Paul brought small cups and a metal tea pot from the kitchen. He offered us some candies and walnuts and poured tea in our cups. The tea looked different from English tea. I took a sip of the black tea with milk and found that it also tasted different from the English tea I was used to. It tasted like milk tea but was a little salty and awful! It was basically tea with a rancid butter taste. I had heard from other friends that *yak* butter tea could taste awful, but somehow, I still felt unprepared for the experience. I thank the Lord that our team did not show our disgust and handled it well. Later, after a few trips to that region, I discovered that a small candy in the mouth could cover the taste of the rancid butter. Our host described to us how their local *yak* butter tea was carefully prepared. Paul told us his mom and other women in the village used a wooden vessel to churn the yak milk to make it into butter. I also discovered that some older women use the butter as a facial moisturizer. It protects their skin from the harsh weather. Paul showed us another room in the house which they called a family altar. I saw small images of their idols in bronze and silver standing on the altar. There were also posters of idol images. Small baskets of fruit and flowers had been presented there as offerings. Later, Paul offered to show us the village. As we walked outside, we saw some small children who were playing on the dirt road. When the children saw the white-skinned foreigners, they all looked amused and surprised.

As we walked around the village, our team enjoyed the nice view of the mountains, the fields, and the little stream that ran along the side of the village. There were some animals roaming freely on the dirt road – chickens, pigs, and goats. We all enjoyed the visit to the little J'rong village and returned happily via taxi to the town which was about five kilometers away.

Meeting MJ

For I am not ashamed of the Gospel of Christ, for it is the power of God to salvation for everyone who believes... (Romans 1:16)

In the afternoon, from our hotel, our team walked to the western part of the town. We reached a small local school where Daniel told us he would like us to see some middle school students whom he had met a while back. It was 5:00 p.m., closing time, so we saw many children coming out of the school. A group of five young girls emerged, maybe around 13-14 years old, who were excited to see a bunch of white-skinned foreigners. The beautiful young girls had long hair and were wearing blue jeans and denim jackets. They had the most beautiful smiles. Daniel introduced MJ to us, after which he introduced each of her friends. We chit-chatted for a little while, until some of the girls said they had to run back to their homes.

MJ invited us to visit her home. We all walked to her house, which was about two kilometers on the other side of the town. Most people in the town walked to the stores, markets, and shops although there were some local taxis available to drive people to nearby villages outside the town. When we got to the house of MJ, we saw a small shop in front of the house. The girl greeted her mother and they spoke in their local language. MJ then introduced each one of us to her mother – a small, sweet lady who was probably in her late forties. She was wearing traditional J'rong clothing, with a nice colorful apron wrapped over her woolen robe. She also wore traditional J'rong headgear, with her braided hair tied around a black cloth. Her clothing and headgear looked like the traditional clothing we had seen the older women wear in the temple, except that her outfit looked newer and cleaner. Even though we did not know their language, we were able to communicate with smiles, and her daughter did some translation for us, from Chinese to the J'rong language. We learned to say "hello" in their language, *"Tashidelek!"*

MJ and her mother invited us to come inside their little shop where they sold different trinkets, jewelry, purses, and souvenirs – all handmade, with traditional ethnic-style designs. I noticed in the glass cabinet, they also had fabric materials used to make prayer flags, and red, burgundy, and yellow fabrics used for the clothing of religious priests. Prayer flags were assembled from pieces of colored paper with prayers and scriptures in their language printed on them. They were also selling different colorful fabrics used as banners to hang on the *stupas* (altars) in their temples. In addition to those, they were also selling small images and statues of idols made of iron, silver, and gold plate.

Next, I noticed a part of the wall which had posters of idols. They looked like the same images we had seen in the temple and in the house of Paul. The images looked grotesque and scary. Later, when we were together with the team, I made a comment, something like, "I do not understand how they can worship idols that look grotesque and scary."

At the time, I did not understand the culture of that ethnic tribe who worshipped those idols. I realized later that I had made an ignorant comment. I am glad I did not make such comments in front of them. However, my heart was grieved to see the futility of their religion. My heart wanted to say to the J'rong people what Jesus said in the Bible, in John 4:24, "God is Spirit, and those who worship Him must worship in spirit and truth." It reminded me also of the words in Isaiah 44 which talked about the foolishness of idolatry.

He cuts down cedars for himself,
And takes the cypress and the oak;
He secures it for himself among the trees of the forest.
He plants a pine, and the rain nourishes it.
Then it shall be for a man to burn,
For he will take some of it and warm himself;
Yes, he kindles it and bakes bread;
Indeed, he makes a god and worships it;
He makes it a carved image and falls down to it.
He burns half of it in the fire;
With this half he eats meat;
He roasts a roast and is satisfied.
He even warms himself and says,
"Ah! I am warm,
I have seen the fire."
And the rest of it he makes into a god,
His carved image.
He falls down before it and worships it,
Prays to it and says,
"Deliver me, for you are my god!"
(Isaiah 44:14-17)

We enjoyed visiting with MJ's family. We all rejoiced and were blessed by their hospitality and openness to us. After three days, we all rode the public bus to travel back to the mainland. The visiting team went back to the Philippines with a new and rich experience of the different cultures of the mainland Chinese and the ethnic people of the J'rong.

A second trip

After that trip, Daniel and I encouraged the local Han Chinese Christians from the mainland to travel with us to the J'rong region to reach out to another ethnic group with the Gospel of the Lord Jesus. At the end of June 2002, we traveled to the J'rong region with five local Christians from different small church groups.

We maintained the same itinerary that we had with the team from the Philippines. We went to the temple, the home of Paul, and to the store of MJ's family. Then one afternoon, we invited Paul and his friends to eat supper in the town. While in the restaurant, one of our team members told our J'rong friends that we usually pray for our meal. After we prayed for the food, Paul asked, "To which god do you all pray? Who is the god you pray to?"

Their religion of idolatry has many kinds of gods, so Paul asked his questions sincerely and with curiosity. He knew Daniel had a different religion from him, but Paul had not met a Chinese Christian until then. It was a point of interest to him to see the Chinese and the foreigners pray together to the same God. Stephen, being the oldest brother in our group, was asked to share and explain about our faith. With gentleness and kind words, Stephen spoke to Paul, "We pray to our God, we call him Jesus. Would you like to hear about Him?"

So, while eating supper, Stephen explained to Paul salvation through Jesus. And to everyone's surprise, Paul said, "Yes, I want to know your god, Jesus, and I want to believe Him."

We all rejoiced that night! A new brother in the Lord was born. We did not know of any local church in the area, and even if there was, it would have been a handful of Han Chinese Christians. Later, we planned for Paul to be baptized and have discipleship lessons. The challenge was that it was a long way from the mainland to travel to the J'rong region. The 8 to 10-hour road trip through the rugged mountains was not much fun at all, and it was not easy to arrange for Chinese Christians to travel there. Most of them had work, and only during summer or winter breaks were they able to travel. At the same time, by the end of summer of 2002, Daniel's missionary work-term with his organization had finished. The challenge to continue the ministry to the J'rong people was up to the local church on the mainland.

With our training ministry on the mainland, we started to see the need to add an introduction to cross-cultural training with the local church. There was a growing interest, especially among the young believers, to reach out to their own indigenous people. However, it did not come without its challenges. One such challenge was to encourage the local church to learn the new language of the indigenous people. They also had to learn to be sensitive to another culture of their own indigenous people.

A New J'rong Sister

Later, I organized another trip to the J'rong region with some foreign and local friends from the southwest city. We made plans to visit a couple of villages to distribute some toys and candies to the children. This is where we pick up the story of MJ. As you may recall, she was our main tour guide in the village, and she knew a lot of the children and the people in the village.

When MJ asked, "Who is Jesus?" I forgot she may not have heard the story of Jesus. I replied to her, "Jesus is our God in heaven. He is the highest God. He created the sky, the heaven, and the people. He died on the cross for our sins because He loves you and me." There was so much to say about Jesus, I did not know where to begin. Under normal circumstances, when I had a long time for friendship and Bible Study, I would begin with the story of creation, Adam and Eve, sin, and other stories in the Bible. I was aware that MJ did not have any Bible background, nor was she familiar with the Christian story of which many of us in the free world are aware. To my surprise, MJ said, "I want to know your Jesus, and I want to believe Him like you do." I was very surprised and did not expect such a quick move in her heart. So, to be sure that she understood what I was saying to her, I called Natalie, one of the Chinese girls with me, to help. I told Natalie with excitement, "I told MJ about the meaning of the color of the beads and Jesus. She said she wants to believe Jesus. Please make sure she understood what I told her, and that I understood what she told me." They spoke in Chinese for more than a few minutes. I was confident that Natalie was able to offer a better explanation of the Gospel in Chinese. After a long talk, Natalie looked at me and told me in English with a big smile on her face, "Yes Vicki, MJ told me she wants to believe Jesus also."

Our group went back to our hotel very happy and excited, for a new sister in the Lord was born that day. The following day, the Chinese girls in our group invited MJ to our hotel room. We were all discreet since we did not want to draw any attention from other people. Spreading the Gospel in that area, just like in the rest of the country, was restricted. We were all aware that there were Christians who got in trouble or were put in jail for preaching the Gospel. Three of the Chinese girls on our team shared some Bible readings in Chinese with MJ about salvation. It was her first time to see and read the Bible. When asked, she said she wanted to be baptized, so we baptized her in the tub in the bathroom of the hotel room. We saw a new joy on her face. She felt that she was a new person, a child of God from heaven! After giving her a Bible in Chinese, we all went back to the mainland rejoicing in what the Lord had done! She was the second person whom we knew among the J'rong people in their town to become a Christian.

A conflict of faith and tradition

After a few months we made another trip to the same mountainous region to visit our J'rong friends. To my big surprise, I found out that MJ had shared the Good News with four of her friends in school. She could not hide the great news. Her joy and new glow were obvious. Her friends also wanted to believe in Jesus, so she shared with them some readings from the Bible.

However, the sad news was that the family of MJ was not happy that she had changed religions. At that time, in their area, it was unheard of that a J'rong would become a Christian. For them to be a J'rong is to be a worshipper of their idol gods. With concern in her voice, she shared with us her problem: "During a festival, our family usually goes to the temple for worship. We are all required to go and expected to go. I learned from the Bible that Jesus is the True God. What do I do? Should I still worship the idols in the temple? I do not want to upset my family, especially my mother. I think she understands me, but we have elders among our relatives and clan, and in our culture, we have to obey them too."

MJ was confronted with a dilemma with her new faith. So, our team tried to encourage her. We said something like, "The Lord God knows your heart. If you must do your obligation with your family, it is okay. But in your heart, you do not have to worship or pray to those false gods. We will pray for you."

On another trip to the mountain city, with another team from the Philippines and the United States, we visited MJ's family. Her mother was very kind and hospitable to us. We saw MJ sitting next to her mother, showing her affection by stroking her hair and hugging her. MJ shared with our team that her mother had some serious health issues. One of our visiting team members from the USA, Kevin, spoke to MJ's mother through a translator and offered to pray for her. MJ's mother accepted the offer to pray.

After praying for healing, Kevin felt led to speak with her about our God, Jesus, who has the power to heal and who loves them. MJ's mother was listening intently. After Kevin shared, she paused and thought for a while. Then she spoke gently in her J'rong language. MJ translated for us in Chinese, "I know that you are all good people. I think your god is true. I can see the changes in my daughter. I can see that she seems different, and she talks about Jesus a lot. I want to believe in your god, too. But you see, I am old now. All my life my family has only known our traditional religion and our gods." Then she paused, and with almost teary eyes, she said, "I want to believe in your god, but it would be difficult; our relatives and community may not accept it."

We did not press the issue of her believing in Jesus. We prayed for her quietly that the Lord would touch and heal her. Kevin then politely replied to her, "We understand you. We pray that you will get to know our God in heaven someday."

A New Church Is Born

MJ and her friends continued to gather in a small group for Bible study. Paul and his friends joined them, too. Later, Paul had to go to another city for his college education. A couple of his friends continued to join the local fellowship in the mountain city. A few months later, a local Chinese evangelist from the mainland felt called to help the young people of J'rong to grow in their faith and to be their pastor. A year or so later, I moved to another region, to the western plateau, but I felt confident that the new J'rong church was taken care of by the pastor. The local church in the mainland (southwest) continued to send teams to the J'rong region and other areas to reach ethnic people groups with the Gospel.

A couple of years later, I heard that MJ got married to a local young man. I was told that it was an arranged marriage. In their tradition and culture, a young woman when she turns 18 or so, has to be married. Just a few years later, I heard again through friends that MJ had a child, but also got divorced. After I moved to other places, I lost communication with her.

Still later, in 2013, during my visit to the southwest, the Lord made a way for me to reconnect with MJ. We had a joyous reunion! She was still the same bubbly young lady I had met some years before when she was still in middle school. In about ten years, she had become a young mother who had gone through a lot in life, yet she kept her faith. She told me all the things that had happened in her life – her marriage, divorce, and the challenges of raising a child by herself. She told me that she had moved to another city to get a better job. In that city, she was able to share her Christian faith with people of her same ethnicity. However, due to some political disturbance in the area, she had to move back to the southwest. She was able to set up a small business with the help of some friends, making and selling jewelry and other ethnic-made products from her hometown. She also told me that a couple of her sisters had become Christians. MJ surprised me also when she told me that one of the jewelries that she made and sold was like the bracelet with colorful beads that expresses the Gospel story.

"*Jiejie*, do you remember the bracelet with the colorful beads that tells the story of Jesus that you gave me a long time ago?" MJ asked me. I said, "Yes, I remember that." Then she said, "I've been making those bracelets and giving them to other people. I tell them about Jesus whenever I have the opportunity."

I was so delighted that our Lord gave me the opportunity to see MJ again after several years. Even though she had gone through a lot of challenges, she had kept the faith. The Lord has been faithful to her and kept her faith strong. MJ continues to be a light and a witness for Jesus among her people. Before we said good-bye, she gave me a pair of earrings and a bracelet with turquoise beads to remember her by.

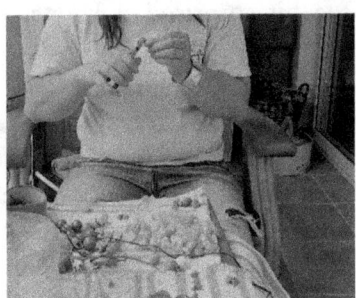

MJ making jewelry beads

Chapter 17: CHRISTMAS TIME!

"Glory to God in the highest, And on earth peace, goodwill toward men!" (Luke 2:14)

It was December 23, 2005, the day before Christmas Eve, in a city in the western plateau. The temperature outside was negative 5^0 C (23^0 F), yet still, the sun was shining bright. I wish it was snowing; instead, it was so cold that it was freezing. Puddles of water on the road turned to ice. Rivers and lakes turned to ice. My body was already acclimatized to the altitude of the city of more than 10,000 feet in height. I was cleaning the living room, trying to tidy up the apartment. I took the small Christmas tree from the box and propped it in a corner next to the TV set. I had the meat and vegetable stew steaming on the stove. I also had some small trinkets as gifts that I had placed on the small Christmas tree. I made plans to invite a couple of local friends to come for Christmas Eve dinner. As I was busy with my preparations, suddenly my cellphone rang.

"Ni hao" (hello), I said to the caller though I did not recognize the number. "Ni hao, Vicki! This is Joma." I was a bit surprised. I had just visited her family about a week or so before. I was not expecting a call from her. After exchanges of *how are you*, she said, "I heard that the Christmas holiday is coming. I have not heard of Christmas before and do not know about it." I felt she was interested, so I extended my invitation to her for the Christmas dinner. I answered her, "Yes, Christmas is a very important holiday for us. Would you like to come and join me tomorrow?

I plan to make a simple meal with a couple of my friends."

Christmas time is my favorite time of the year! Back in the Philippines where I grew up, Christmas is a big holiday. The air is filled with Christmas music and songs as early as September. Shops and stores start to decorate as early as October and November. Many houses and offices have colorful Christmas ornaments – Christmas trees, wreaths, lanterns, and other ornaments. Schools and offices have Christmas parties and programs beginning in the month of December. Churches and small groups have different activities for Christmas such as concerts, musicals, cantatas, Christmas plays, games, etc. There are many family reunions and friends gathering here and there. It is truly a festive season!

Children go Christmas caroling as early as the first week of December until Christmas Eve. Bunches of children go from house to house with their makeshift musical instruments, made of wire and bottle caps, accompanied by a small ukulele or tin cans as a drum. Children sing simple Christmas carols, such as Jingle Bells, and other Christmas songs they know from memory or have heard on the radio. At most homes, the children are given a few coins or candies as an expression of thanks. I, too, went caroling when I was small. As an adult, it was a joy to see some children continuing the tradition. Growing up, my family did not have much, but we always celebrated Christmas as the most important holiday because it is the birth of Jesus and a tradition!

When I moved to China, in the southwest city, I was aware that Christmas was not celebrated the way it was in my home country. That was one of my adjustments: that Christmas was only an ordinary day. I saw people go to work and children go to school. It was a big contrast coming from the country where I grew up. I missed the Christmas traditions that I had grown up with. I had to remind myself that Christmas is not about me; it is the birthday of my Lord Jesus after all. So even though I missed the festive Christmas celebration, I had to do my part to make known to others the true meaning of Christmas.

For the Christian community, foreign and local, Christmas was the best time for us to share the Gospel, especially for those who have not heard the real story of the first Christmas, the birth of our Lord Jesus. The local Christians in the southwest, though they were a minority – just a handful during the late 1990s to the early 2000s – celebrated the Christmas holiday in their own private way. Some of the house churches rented a room in a tea house, or restaurant, for a private party or program. Members of those small groups were encouraged to bring some friends or family members. I heard from some friends that during the Christmas celebrations and presentations of the Gospel, many local people received the Christmas story and the love of Jesus Christ gladly.

Together with my other foreign friends, we prepared small Christmas dinners and invited our non-believer friends to share our Christmas celebration and the true meaning of Christmas. Some of our Chinese friends came out of curiosity to experience what they thought was a western holiday. Many of the locals who had had no exposure to Christianity said that Christmas was an American or Western holiday. Some even called Christmas "Lao Ren Jie," which means in English "Old Man's Holiday," referring to Santa Claus. However, those who became Christians celebrated Christmas as a very special day celebrating the birth of our Savior, the Lord Jesus Christ.

In my few years in the country, the Lord blessed me with some fun memories of Christmas celebrations with friends from my Sunday fellowship and a few local friends. My first Christmas celebration was with my team from the Philippines. One weekend night before Christmas Day, we invited about five local friends from the college. We had a Bible study, sang, played some games, and had a meal together. It was the first time for these local friends to experience a Christmas celebration.

After that, I had other fun memories of Christmas celebrations with friends in China. I saw doors open for opportunities to share a very important part of my culture and my faith with local friends.

One other memorable Christmas celebration was during my last term in the country (2011-2013) when I served in the northeast part of the country. I was part of a local church in the big city. The church made plans to have a huge Christmas tree right outside the church building. On that Sunday evening, about two days before Christmas day, we had a big program with choirs singing and a message about Christmas. It was a big thing for me, since we were outside the church building right on the street, where some people passing by saw the Christmas celebration. For about an hour, we were standing outside shivering in the cold night. When the lights on the Christmas tree were turned on, to the witness of a couple of hundred people, I praised the Lord with teary eyes. It was an amazing moment for me to see the local church experience a small degree of freedom for that moment to celebrate Christmas openly.

Another memorable Christmas

For God so loved the world that He gave His only begotten Son, that whoever believes in Him should not perish but have everlasting life. (John 3:16)

After seven years in the southwest city, the Lord blessed me with a unique and rare opportunity to serve with a Medical Project in another province. My good American friend, Marlene, and I arrived in the southwest city at almost the same time in 1997. We met and became friends in Sunday Fellowship. Later, we also became housemates as we shared an apartment in the city. In 2004, she moved to a city in the western plateau of the country.

In the Spring of 2005, Marlene invited me to join her work in a medical project. We organized treatments for children from the region who had congenital heart disease. Volunteer doctors and surgeons came from the big city of Beijing and the country of Japan. Some of the children underwent open-heart surgeries, while others received stents. A few of the families came from villages in the higher plateau who had come to receive free medical treatment since most of them were not able to afford such expensive procedures. There were times when we had to bring some families to the capital city (Beijing) where there were better medical facilities and technology.

The first phase of the medical project was a screening process at a local hospital in the main city. The workers at the hospital helped us determine which village had the most need for medical attention. One time, Marlene and I, along with some workers from the local hospital, drove for about six hours to another county in the region. We visited an elementary school in a village that was at a higher elevation, about 14,000 feet above sea level. (The region is known as The Rooftop of the World.) Many of the people in the village were farmers and herders. During that screening, we did some medical check-ups with about 400-500 children in the school. From those children, nearly 100 were found with congenital heart disease. We explained to the parents and teachers that our medical project offered free medical treatment. We then waited for the parents to decide whether they would like to avail of such a wonderful opportunity for their children's health and life. A lot of them accepted the offer, but there were a few who did not accept our offer. We were told that some, for religious reasons, decided not to take the medical treatment offered to them.

Most of the people in that region practice a traditional religion of worshipping idols. They usually consult their traditional priest for such big decisions. Some of them said that their priests had told them that it was not good for their children to receive medical treatment because it was their fate, that is, the sickness was their fate.

The second phase of the medical project was to facilitate the process of arranging surgeries for the children who were found to have severe congenital heart disease during the screening procedure. The people in that region in the western plateau of the country live mostly at high elevations from 8,000 feet to 17,000 feet. Perhaps due to lack of oxygen and poor health conditions in the area, many children were born with heart disease or lung disease. In addition, most of the people in that region are indigenous and lived in isolated mountain areas where medical facilities are inaccessible.

In the summer of 2005, Marlene and I organized the medical project by coordinating with the doctors and the parents. Our medical team from Beijing and Japan came for a few days and performed heart surgeries for the children. Several children received stents to close holes in the heart or to repair other heart defects. Most of them were from four to fourteen years of age.

We thank the Lord that most of the surgeries went well. However, some children had conditions requiring open-heart surgeries. In those cases, we had to travel to the mainland for the open-heart surgery.

A hospital in Beijing partnered with the medical project to facilitate the medical procedures.

In the fall of 2005, Marlene and I travelled to Beijing to help the families receive these medical procedures for their children. Our medical project provided transportation and lodging for each child and a parent. We helped them with the registration and all the arrangements from the day they arrived at the hospital to the day they checked out from the hospital. We also facilitated important communications between the medical doctors and the parents. Often, conversation was difficult since most of the families came from an ethnic group that spoke their own local language, which was not Mandarin Chinese. With the help of translation, Marlene and I were able to communicate with the families.

The medical project we worked with was under a Christian organization from the USA. The founding-director had the special privilege of being invited by a local official of the western plateau to provide heart surgeries for the children in the region. The organization had raised a lot of funds to save lives of many children whose families were not able to afford such medical treatment. Many of those children would not live long enough to be adults if they did not receive medical treatment. For the two years I was part of the medical project, we saw more than two hundred children receive critical heart surgeries. We saw how their health and lives were greatly improved. We saw the joy and the sense of relief on the face of each parent after the surgeries were completed.

Marlene and I were open with the local staff of the hospital that we were Christians. Although the medical doctors and surgeons were not Christians, we expressed to them many times that we pray to our God during each surgery. During some surgeries, there were times the surgeons would let us know that they were not sure if the surgery would be successful or not, especially if the child had a complicated case. Marlene and I would tell them, "We'll be here to pray to our God."

Whenever we had the opportunity, before a child went into the operating room, Marlene and I prayed silently for the child. Then as soon as the surgery started, either Marlene or I, or sometimes the two of us, stayed with the parents outside the operating room. We saw in each parent the fear, worry, and uncertainty. Some mothers were in tears while praying to their traditional gods using their prayer beads. Marlene and I managed to express our care for each of the parents. We usually asked the parents, "Could we pray for you and your child? We pray to our God; His name is Jesus."

We did not make long explanations, but most of the parents gladly received the offer of prayer. This was unique because almost none of them had heard of the God named Jesus. They had different names for their false gods or idols, but sad to say, they had not heard the name of Jesus. With our language limitations, it was a challenge to talk with the families about God or Jesus. To my surprise most of them had no clue and had not even heard of Christianity, nor even the concept of Christmas. It was a real challenge to know where to start sharing about Christianity or the concept of a God in heaven who came to earth and died on the cross for our sins.

After each surgery, during the recovery period of about seven to ten days, we had the opportunity to have more interaction with the parents and the children. We tried to take that time to talk and share with each family about our faith, to tell them about Jesus.

One of the families that came to the medical project was a young mother with her small daughter. When we saw her small child, she looked frail, and her skin color looked purplish. According to the doctors that did her screening, the heart condition of the little girl was severe and needed the medical procedure as soon as possible. The little girl was about five years old, however she looked smaller, like a two-year-old. So, together with the other children who needed heart surgeries, we arranged for them to travel from the western plateau to the mainland city of Beijing, a distance of about 2,300 miles. To take a flight was about five hours with a connecting flight in the southwest city. (A year later, the train system was opened, but it was still at least a 50-hour train ride through the rugged mountains.)

We had about ten children with their parents who traveled from the western plateau to the mainland. As I said before, when we arrived in

Beijing, Marlene and I made all the arrangements at the hospital for the treatment of the children.

All these children had good surgeries, thank the Lord. However, after a couple of days, during the post-operative and recovery period in the intensive care unit, this little girl was not doing well. The doctors informed us and the parents that the little girl might not have a chance to survive. Marlene and I prayed for the little girl, but it seems God had other plans. After another couple of days, sad to say, the little girl passed away. Words cannot express the grief and sorrow that Marlene and I felt for the parents.

The husband of the young mother joined her from their hometown in the western plateau. They decided to cremate their daughter and travel back to their hometown with her urn. Since I had to be with the other families in the hospital, Marlene went with the parents of the little girl to the cremation. Marlene shared with me later the unusual experience that she had during the funeral and cremation of the little child. According to Marlene, after the little girl was cremated, the parents wanted to take home the remains, but the mother struggled to go into the cremation room. Marlene wanted to help them by showing her deep sympathy in a practical way, so she helped the father pick the little bones out of the ashes. It was these bones that the family would keep. Marlene shared with me the deep emotion that she felt at that time. In the natural, she would have "freaked out" to do something like picking up the remains of a dead child. But she so felt the grace and love of God in her that she was able to help the parents. She also saw how much the parents' love could enable them to do such a thing for their child.

After the funeral, Marlene and I decided to switch places. I planned to return to our home base in the western plateau to take care of "the office stuff," while she planned to go to Beijing to be with the families. So, I took a flight from Beijing to the city in the western plateau with a stopover in the city in the southwest where I had lived in the past. I decided to stay there in the southwest city for a few days to visit some old friends and see how the ministry was going with the local church.

After a few days visit in the southwest city, I headed to the airport to fly back to my home base in the western plateau. While at the airport gate waiting for my flight, I saw a couple among the passengers who looked familiar. It was the parents of the little girl who had passed away. They were also returning from Beijing to the same city in the western plateau, on the same flight. It was good to see and talk with them. I noticed that the mother was carrying a little box wrapped with a big, white scarf. I found out that the box contained the ashes of their little girl. I cannot describe what I felt and how surreal that experience was for me. During the flight, as I watched the parents of the little girl who had passed away, memories came back to me.

Just two months prior to that, we were all traveling in a plane from a city in the western plateau to the big city of Beijing. In my memory, I saw the parents and the children traveling with me in the airplane. They all looked excited and anxious at the same time. Most of them had never been to the big city of Beijing. Most of them looked hopeful, including the mom of this little girl. She was carrying her little girl in her arms with a look of hope that her little girl would be better.

Now, after only two months, I was sitting next to the same mom with her little girl in her arms, but she was already reduced to ashes in a little box. I wanted to think that the little girl was with Jesus although the parents were idol worshippers.

Indeed, Marlene and I both believed the little girl really was with Jesus, and that she was not sick anymore – no more pain and sickness. *"Take heed that you do not despise one of these little ones, for I say to you that in heaven their angels always see the face of My Father who is in heaven." (Matthew 18:10).* But how could we explain that to her family who had not heard of the hope that believers know and have in Jesus? We had no words to say.

After almost a whole day's journey, we all arrived in the city in the western plateau. A week later, I visited the young mother of the little girl who passed away. I had learned earlier that the mother's name was Joma. I was relieved to see that she had another daughter. She seemed to be a normal busy mom. I wanted to know how she was doing. She was still sad, but she seemed not to be bitter or upset. I was concerned that she might have been upset by the way things turned out. Maybe if we had not offered the surgery to her daughter, she would still be alive.

However, even the doctors and surgeons told us before the surgery that the condition of the little girl was serious and severe. They were not sure of her chances. I think the parents were aware of that, but they wanted to give their daughter a chance to have the surgery, to give her an opportunity to live. In their economic condition, as with the other families, they had no way to afford such a surgery for their daughter. So, they took the risk in the hopes that the little girl's life would be better. As I talked with other parents, I learned that some of them had lost young children to heart disease.

During the earlier phone conversation with Joma that I mentioned at the start of this chapter, I had asked her if she would like to come to celebrate Christmas with two other friends of mine from the hospital. I did not expect she would come now, but when I asked her on the phone about coming to the dinner, she said, "I would like to come."

The following day, Christmas Eve, the apartment was decorated with a Christmas tree and ornaments. I made a simple meal even though I did not have the traditional meal we used to have in the Philippines for Christmas. One of the two ladies from the hospital was a young lady who worked at the pharmacy. We had become good friends and had done some language study together. I had introduced her to the Bible and to the Christian faith in the past. The other lady was a friend of Marlene's who was our neighbor and a doctor at the hospital. To my surprise, Joma also came! My experience in the past with the locals was that when I invited them for a meal or a visit, they might say they would come, but often they ended up not coming. There were other times when they would say that they were not sure about coming, but they came. I was also surprised to see that Joma brought a gift for me as a Christmas present. She brought the nicest gift in their culture, a big red box with a small replica of a golden calf! In their culture and religion, the golden calf symbolizes blessing or good luck. Some maybe even worship the golden calf. Basically, I was given an idol image as a Christmas gift!

The other friends who worked in the hospital brought some gifts too. We ate dinner, and I shared with them the Christmas story. Many of the people in that city had not heard of Jesus, nor even Christmas. I shared and read the story of Christmas to them. I asked someone to read the passage in the Chinese Bible. Even though they were from another ethnic group and spoke their local dialect, they also spoke and read the Chinese language since their education was all in the Chinese language. At the end of the Christmas story, I told them that Jesus is the real reason for the celebration of Christmas and that Jesus is the True God. I asked them if they wanted to believe and receive Jesus into their hearts. Again, to my big surprise, Joma, the mom who was still mourning the death of her beloved daughter, said that she wanted to believe in Jesus!

The other ladies had already heard the story of Jesus but seeing Joma open her heart to Jesus was surprising to me since I thought she was still grieving the passing away of her little child. However, seeds of faith had already been planted in her heart. Marlene had shared with me that she had told Joma and her husband about the love of Jesus when they were in the hospital. I also believe that the kindness Marlene and I had shown them became the seed of the Gospel. Marlene had shown them the love of God when she helped the father pick up the remains of their little child. Her genuine care and concern opened the door for Joma to believe in our God in heaven. I did not see Joma again after that since I had to travel to the Philippines after Christmas and then back to Beijing for a few months. I did not know of a local Christian church in the city. At that time in 2005, I heard there were a handful of local Christians in the city, maybe fewer than a dozen people! They were very secretive, too, so we were not able to connect Joma to a local church. I regret that I was not able to meet with her for a follow-up Bible study since my time in the region was short. But I prayed that the seed of the Gospel that had been planted in her would be watered by the Lord.

A village in the western plateau region

Children receiving medical treatments

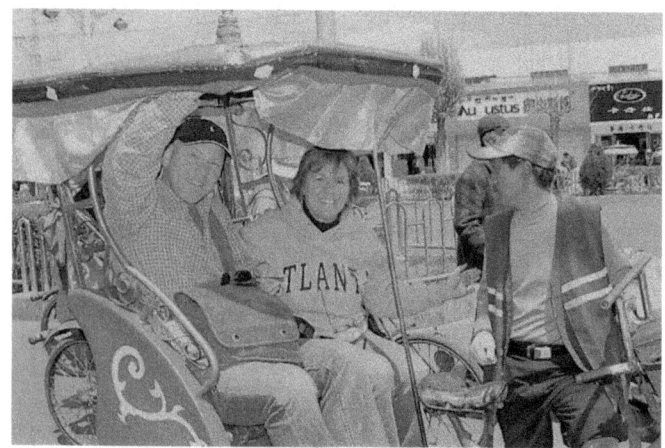

Dr. and Mrs. Quinley's visit to the western plateau in 2006

Chapter 18: SPECIAL FRIENDS

Therefore, whoever humbles himself as this little child is the greatest in the kingdom of heaven. (Matthew 18:4)

In the spring of 2011, after five years of being away, the Lord opened a door for me to again visit China. As I felt led to serve with a children's home, an old friend helped get me connected to a group that operates a children's home in a big metropolitan city in the northeastern part of the country.

During my first visit, a staff worker gave me a tour of the place. When I got to the main playroom area, I saw several children, one to seven years old. Some were playing while others were having physical therapy sessions with some women. In the corner of the big room, I saw a little girl about seven years old; she looked cute with her two pig tails. I observed for a few minutes that she repeatedly rubbed her eyes and face. I was told that she was blind, deaf, and mute. Then I observed the other children, mostly blind boys and girls, rocking their heads or rubbing their faces, repeatedly.

Seeing the playroom full of children who were handicapped, my heart melted. I asked, "Lord, why do these children suffer? What is the purpose of their lives?"

Just like any other person with a compassionate heart, my heart broke when I first saw the children with their physical disabilities: blind, lame, deaf, autistic. Some even had multiple disabilities: blind with autism, cerebral palsy, blind with ADHD, etc. I almost questioned why the Lord created those children. For a few days, I pondered why those children had to suffer. Up to that point, I had believed that God had a plan and a purpose for each person's life. I believed God's Word in Jeremiah 29:11, that He has a good plan for my life and for others who believe in Him.

I also thought that each person's life has a meaning and a purpose, whether a person is a Christian or not. I thought that each life could contribute to his family, community, or society whether he is a doctor, a teacher, a construction worker, a mother, or a school student. Even a garbage collector or a street cleaner could still contribute something for the good of his or her community and society. So, I struggled and grappled with finding meaning and purpose for the lives of those children.

Looking back, I have always enjoyed working with children's ministries. How did I start? I first started working with children in my first church in the Philippines from 1989 to 1995. As I mentioned in the first part of this book, I was part of a team that pioneered a church. We had a small church that rented space in an open pavilion. Since we did not have a proper church building and classrooms, we gathered the children outside the pavilion, under the trees. I served along with my good friend in the children's ministry. We taught the children Bible stories and some children's songs. Vacation Bible School during summer was always fun. It was a joy to see the children grow up knowing that Jesus loved them.

In 2008, I had the privilege of serving at a children's home in Bolivia. I was thankful to the Lord for the ministry of SIFAT (Servants in Faith and Technology in Alabama) for giving me the opportunity to be part of their ministry in the continent of South America. For eight months I served helping children in a boarding home. As SIFAT workers, we provided food, shelter, and care for the children, as well as training in agriculture, gardening, housework, English lessons, and computer skills. We also provided spiritual care as we taught them Bible lessons.

Having had some experience working with children in the Philippines, China, and Bolivia, I gained some appreciation of the love of Jesus for children. I enjoyed working, studying, and playing with the children. I realized whatever culture, language, and background children have, most of them share the same openness to God and to spiritual things. I began to understand a bit better Jesus' words, *"Assuredly I say to you, unless you are converted and become as little children, you will by no means enter the kingdom of heaven. Therefore, whoever humbles himself as this little child is the greatest in the kingdom of God." (Matthew 18:3-4)*

Jesus also warned, *"But whoever causes one of these little ones who believe in Me to sin, it would be better for him if a millstone were hung around his neck, and he were drowned in the depths of the sea." (Matthew 18:6)*

After my first visit to the children's home, I met with the founding directors and was thrilled to be accepted as part of the staff. I returned to the Philippines for several months to process the work visa. I did not know it would take many months. During that time of waiting, the Lord gave me opportunity to learn more about special needs children. A ministry in the Philippines called *Resources for the Blind* allowed me to visit and volunteer in their school for the blind. It was very practical hands-on training with special needs children. It helped me to understand more about the children in that situation. After a few months of volunteer work with *Resources for the Blind*, I finally got my visa to return to China. The Lord also sent me Celeste, a Filipino missionary, to go with me. With a limited visa, she served with me in the Children's Home for only three months.

When I started working, I was able to observe the children more closely to see their daily routine. The house parents took care of their bedding, helped them get dressed, and walked them to the dining hall to be fed. The house parents also took care of giving them exercise and therapy. Some children with physical disabilities who had higher mental capabilities were able to attend classroom teaching – learning how to read and write, mostly in braille. Some of the older children learned to speak and understand English through the help of some foreign volunteers and guests.

Some children, if able, received training in some simple life skills like folding clothes, making their beds, brushing their teeth, or washing their faces. We tend to think that these are basic things in life that everybody knows how to do. However, for these children with physical disabilities, such everyday chores could be challenging. Some of them also received training from one of the volunteer workers on how to use a walking stick properly. However, a few children were unable to take care of themselves, especially those with cerebral palsy or severe autism.

A little boy named Dong Qiang was one of the children who had severe cerebral palsy and was unable to care for himself. I was surprised when I found out that he was about eight to nine years old. I thought he was four or five years old since he was usually propped up in a toddler's stroller. He was not able to speak, but perhaps he could see a little or hear a little. He usually smiled when we touched his face. Often, he looked like he was in pain. The house mothers usually gave him massage therapy in the mornings and afternoons. One of the volunteers who came to the children's home was Ana Marie from Florida. She was skilled and experienced as a nurse and had a heart for children who were severely handicapped. She loved the little boy, Dong Qiang. She was able to help and train the house mothers on how to properly care for him. She also recommended they get a special wheelchair for Dong Qiang since he was too old to be in a toddler's stroller. The Lord provided one through a company that manufactured a custom-made wheelchair for Dong Qiang so that he was more comfortable. We saw some improvement in his countenance as he enjoyed moving about in that special chair. For about a year, Ana Marie also helped take care of children who got sick with stomach illnesses, fever, flu, etc. She was a big help to the children's home and became a good friend of mine. One time, we traveled together to another city on a train for 12 hours. We visited another branch of the children's home and checked on the children there.

I was hired to provide life skills and spiritual oversight for the children. My personal goal was to help the children know Jesus and to know His love for them. The Lord gave me creative ways to share Biblical truths and Bible stories using a book called, *Character First*. From the book we learned lessons on Truthfulness, Courage, Kindness, Love, and other character traits.

One time I had a class with small children – about five to seven years old. The lesson was on the character of *Faith*. I shared the story of Abraham who demonstrated the character of faith when God made a promise to him. I told the children that God told Abraham, *"Look now toward heaven and count the stars if you are able to number them." And He said to him, "So shall your descendants be." (Genesis 15:5)*

So, with enthusiasm I said to the children, "There were many, many stars in the sky. They looked bright and colorful!" Then one of the little boys, Lulu, spoke in Chinese and said, "But Laoshi (teacher), we are blind, we can't see the stars!" "Oh, yes! I am sorry, Lulu."

I guess I almost forgot that they were blind. Sometimes, as much as possible, I tried to treat those children like other normal children. For their activity, we made paper stars. I prepared cutout paper in the shape of stars. They happily smothered the paper stars with glitter and glue. With that activity of touching the shape of a star, and touching the glitter, the children were able to connect to the lesson. They also memorized some sayings from the lesson.

When appropriate, I was able to share with some of the children about Jesus on a personal basis during times when we talked or played.

Life in the city

A few older children, ages eight to twelve who were blind but had normal mental capacities, were moved to an apartment in the big city. They went to a public school for the blind and were taught some life skills, with the hope that someday they could manage on their own. The house mothers assisted the children in the homes and walked them to the school. On weekends, I visited them, played games, and shared Bible stories. I also arranged some fun activities for them. One Saturday, with the help of some volunteers from a local church, we went to a park and did fishing. Another time, we went to the zoo. Although the children were not able to see much, they were able to touch and smell the fish in the pond and hear the animals in the zoo. They also enjoyed riding the subway train and walking on the streets, since they could hear people around them.

One of the children in that program was Dong Fang. He was about ten years old and totally blind. At the same time, he also struggled with ADHD (Attention Deficit Hyperactive Disorder) and had a bit of difficulty walking with his deformed feet. Some of the house mothers had a challenge in keeping up with his hyper activeness. When he was not doing anything, he usually fiddled with something or repeatedly knocked his head on the table or the wall. Another co-worker who was the psychologist for the children and I tried to assist the house mothers in understanding and managing Dong Fang's ADHD symptoms.

A few times the house mothers had told me that some of Dong Fang's teachers had made complaints about him. According to the teachers, Dong Fang had difficulty paying attention in class. A couple of times, he managed to slip out from the classroom. Sometimes they found him walking up and down the stairs of the school building. I observed that even though Dong Fang had physical challenges, he had a brilliant mind.

One time I came to their apartment to have lessons with the children. Dong Fang came to me, and said, "Laoshi, (teacher) come, listen to this!" He took my hand and brought it to his chest and said, "Hear this, Jesus is in my heart! He is inside of me!" I heard him say that more than a couple of times that day. I was thrilled and said to Dong Fang, "Yes, Jesus lives in your heart and He loves you Dong Fang!" I had prayed too, for the Lord's grace to be upon him, and for understanding for the teachers. I thank the Lord that he was not kicked out from the class and the school.

Another child in that apartment in the city was Lili. She was about 9 years old and had been in the children's home for almost five years. One time during my visits, I mentioned to the children the love of Jesus. I was a bit taken a back when Lili said, "I don't think Jesus cares for me." I replied to her, "Why did you say that? You know Jesus loves you!" Lili replied, "If Jesus cares for me, why am I blind and an orphan?" My heart sank. I did not know what to say or how to answer her question. I do not remember much of what I explained to her, but I did tell her, "But Jesus still loves you, Lili!"

In my first few months after coming to the children's home, I found out that the paperwork for Lili's adoption was in process. I had heard that it takes at least a year to process the documents. A few weeks later, Lili was informed that she had a new family coming to adopt her. Lili got excited! One time I told Lili, "See Lili, Jesus loves you so much that He is giving you a new family!" Lili smiled and said something like, "Ah, hmm."

A week later her new parents arrived from the USA. They spent a week together and traveled to her old hometown. First, they had to get paperwork from her original orphanage. Then they came back to the children's home to collect her stuff and to say goodbye to everyone. I saw Lili beaming and full of joy! The house parents and teachers of the foster home, together with all the children, gave her a big farewell party. Lili was so happy, but at the same time, she was in tears when she said goodbye to her house mothers whom she had called "Mama" since she was a child. She was sad to say goodbye to her brothers and sisters in the foster home. She was sad to say goodbye to the Papa and Mama she knew growing up who were the founders of the foster home. I was sad to see Lili go, but in my heart, I was rejoicing with her to see that Jesus had blessed her with a family of her own. Before Lili left, I found a few minutes with her. I gave her a big hug and said, "Lili you know Jesus loves you, for He is giving you a new family!" Lili replied with a smile on her face, "Yes, now I know!"

In the 14 months I was at the children's home, I saw several children who were adopted by new families, mostly from the USA. It was usually a bittersweet sight for me. I saw that the happiest day for a child was the day they got to be with their new families. I could almost feel their excitement. However, it was also sad to see them go. I witnessed both the sad and happy moments as a child said goodbye to their *laoshi* (teachers), house parents, the staff, and the other children that they had known as their brothers, sisters, and friends. At the same time, as some children left for their new homes and families, there were new children who came to the foster home from other orphanages. There were new children to take care of and help.

Most of the workers and staff in the children's home treated the children with dignity, respect, and love. The children might look pitiful in the eyes of the world, with their physical disabilities, but they were still children created in the image of God. Going back to my questions, *"Why do these children suffer? What is the purpose of God in their lives?* I may not have all the answers, but one thing I felt the Lord taught me during my time with the special needs children was unconditional love. ***The purpose of God in the lives of these children was to teach me what it means to love unconditionally. I learned to love those children without any rewards or returns, as those children were not capable of doing much for themselves. God taught me a valuable lesson of loving without expecting anything in return.*** God loves them as they are and cares for them too, as He cares for you and me. Even though their own parents may have abandoned them, God made a way for those children to come to that children's home and be cared for.

In 2013, due to some unforeseen circumstances, after almost two years of working with the children's home, I had to leave my post. The last activity I had with the children in the city was in the winter of 2013. With six children we went to a nearby park, which was like a ski resort as the lake turned to ice during the cold of winter. Again, with the help of volunteers, the children enjoyed riding on sledges as they slid on the ice. We also enjoyed activities like fishing and visiting the zoo as we had done before.

Then with a very heavy heart, I said goodbye to the children and to the staff and workers. I moved back to the Philippines, and shortly after that, the Lord led me to come back to the USA with Servants in Faith and Technology (SIFAT).

In the spring of 2017, I found out several of them are now living in the USA with their adoptive families. My heart is rejoicing and praising our Lord that those children now have their own "forever families" who love and care for them. God is truly good and faithful! Psalm 68:5 says that God is "A *Father to the fatherless.*"

Children in Bolivia

SIFAT Bolivia - Children's Home in Xiamas, Bolivia

Computer lessons with children in Bolivia

Children's Home in China

Children's Home in China

Playing with the sledge on the ice with the children

Only If They Know

Only if they know You
Only if they know
How much you love them,
They will love you too
Only if they know your love
They too will be in awe of You.
Only if they know
That You gave Your all
Body, soul, and all
Only if they know
That Your body was bruised for our transgression
Only if they know
You bore a crown of thorns
Only if they know
You carried the cross for our sins
Only if they know
Your hands and feet were nailed to the cross for our iniquities
Only if they know
Jesus, only if they know
They too will be in awe
That You love them so true
Jesus, if they know
How much you love them so
They too will love you so.

PART 3:

DAVID CALLED TO THE HARVEST FIELD

How then shall they call on Him in whom they have not believed? And how shall they believe in Him of whom they have not heard? And how shall they hear without a preacher? And how shall they preach unless they are sent? As it is written: "How beautiful are the feet of those who preach the gospel of peace, Who bring glad tidings of good things!" But they have not all obeyed the gospel. For Isaiah says, "LORD, who has believed our report?" So, then faith comes by hearing, and hearing by the word of God. But I say, have they not heard? Yes indeed: 'Their sound has gone out to all the earth, And their words to the ends of the world."
(Romans 10:14-18)

Chapter 19: DAVID'S STORY

The following story is taken from David's speaking notes during church visits in 2014.

Greetings! My name is David Creel. I was born in Birmingham, Alabama. I am the son of the late Rev. & Mrs. George Creel who served several United Methodist churches here in Northern Alabama.

As you can imagine, being the son of a United Methodist pastor, I grew up in church. I don't ever remember a time when I wasn't in church. Every time the church doors were open, I was there. I really didn't have a choice. I might not have appreciated it at the time, but I am so grateful now for my parents' insistence on church attendance. I am also eternally grateful for the godly example that my mom and dad provided for me and my sisters as we grew up.

As a child, I usually slept during church. Frankly, I still have some trouble if I've been out late the night before, but I don't think I'm alone in that confession! My mom could tell you about a time as a child when I had fallen asleep on the pew during an evening service. Everyone went home, the lights were turned off, and I wasn't discovered to be missing until a short time later! I, on the other hand, was clueless – still asleep on the pew!

Around the age of 10, I began noticing that my friends were sitting up and paying attention, so I decided that I needed to do the same. It was around that time that I realized that my parents' relationship with God did not guarantee that I was right with Him. I needed my own personal relationship with Jesus Christ, the one who gave His life on Calvary so that I might spend eternity in heaven with Him.

I distinctly remember hearing the gospel clearly presented by my dad one Sunday morning: how Jesus died for my sins, and how I needed to ask him for forgiveness, and invite Him into my heart. I did not go forward during the invitation. However, I promised myself that I would go forward the next Sunday. During the invitation on November 24, 1968, I made my way to the altar at Walker Memorial United Methodist Church in Birmingham and was saved.

Here is a quote from my dad's journal on that day: "David saved! Thank God...this morning, my son David made his way to the altar, alone, to be saved. Jesus faithfully saved him as he wept his confession to God. Hallelujah...I couldn't speak further. Granville (our choir director) dismissed the congregation. Thank you, Jesus forever!"

Although I was saved at that time, I really didn't do the things one needs to do to grow as a Christian. Sure, I still went to church, but I didn't really spend much time in Bible study and prayer. Just as in the physical realm, one must eat in order to grow, so it is in the spiritual realm. In I Peter 2:2, we are told, "like newborn babes, long for the pure milk of the word, that by it you may grow in respect to salvation..." It wasn't until a few years later that I realized the importance of this fact and did what it took to grow as a Christian.

But, even at this early age, I believe that God was preparing me for missionary service. I learned electronics by observing Dad's repair of antique radios. Many a spare moment was spent with my dad in the basement working on his latest project. I went with Dad to WDJC-FM in Birmingham where he preached on a couple of radio programs. Through these visits, I became friends with the station's chief engineer and developed a keen interest in radio. On one of the trips to WDJC, we stopped at the Baptist Bookstore where I picked up a copy of the book *Skywaves* which told the story of how a mission organization called Far East Broadcasting Company was using shortwave radio to broadcast the Good News of Jesus Christ to far-away lands. This book further "sparked my interest" in radio as a possible career.

Around this time, I built my own small AM radio station using a low power transmitter obtained from a gentleman at the local electronics store. I also developed an interest in amateur radio and received a license at the age of 13.

During my high school years, I drifted away from my commitment to Christ. Although I never did anything terrible – just the usual teenage stuff – I was still rebelling against God. The best way to describe those years was a *roller coaster* experience. I wanted to live for Christ, especially after a particularly good youth retreat, but never had the power to *follow through* with a consistent walk with the Lord. I tried to be a *fence walker* with one foot in the church and the other in the things of the world. I wanted to *talk the talk* of being a Christian but didn't have the power to *walk the walk*.

Just before my senior year in high school, God used several events to *get my attention* including a couple of car wrecks and a move from Sheffield to Gadsden. The move to Gadsden, just as I was about to begin my senior year, was particularly hard to accept. But even this was a part of God's wonderful plan for my life.

During my senior year, I really got tired of my *roller coaster* Christian experience, but I didn't know how to change myself or the situation. I began to earnestly pray and seek God for the answer. A devotional book that I had been reading mentioned how the Holy Spirit can help us live the Christian life. Shortly thereafter, our church had a "Lay Witness Mission." This was a weekend event where ordinary lay people (not preachers) came and shared what God had done in their lives. During this event, I heard several people share how Christ must not only be our Savior, but He must also be Lord of every aspect of our lives. I also heard a lot about Acts 1:8, "But you shall receive power when the Holy Spirit has come upon you; and you shall be witnesses to Me in Jerusalem, and in all Judea and Samaria, and to the end of the earth."

On Sunday, October 12, 1975, I rededicated my life to Christ, allowing Him to be Lord of my life, and asked God to fill me with the Holy Spirit and to help me live a consistent Christian life. This He did! He gave me a new desire to read and study His Word and to pray during a daily quiet time. He also provided some wonderful Christian friends to help me in my spiritual journey. I learned much about the Bible from my dad and benefited greatly from the example and encouragement provided by both Mom and Dad.

Has my life been perfect or without sin since that time? As a missionary, do I *have it all together*? Of course not. Just like everyone else, I am a sinner *saved by grace* and sometimes have struggles. But, with the help of the Holy Spirit, I have been able to live a much more consistent Christian life since allowing Christ to be Lord of my life. The verse that I feel best describes the way to live a Christian life is Galatians 2:20, "*I have been crucified with Christ; it is no longer I who live, but Christ lives in me; and the life which I now live in the flesh I live by faith in the Son of God, who loved me and gave Himself for me.*"

Just after my high school graduation, I was invited to go on a short-term mission trip to Haiti. This experience really helped me to see *first-hand* the needs of people in impoverished lands. I began to sense that perhaps God was calling me to be a missionary – but not in the traditional sense. I was fascinated by the idea of using high power shortwave radio to tell the people of the world about our Lord and Savior Jesus Christ. I felt that God was calling me to be a technical missionary.

With missions in mind, I enrolled in the pre-engineering program at Gadsden State Junior College. I later transferred to Auburn University where I majored in Electrical Engineering. God also provided a cooperative education job with Alabama Power Company in Gadsden to help cover the costs of my college education.

During this time, I made my second short-term mission trip – this time to a shortwave radio station, HCJB, in Quito, Ecuador. This trip further strengthened my conviction that I was to be a missionary engineer.

Upon graduation from college, the door to missionary service did not immediately open so, I accepted a job as an engineer with Alabama Power Company in Oneonta, Alabama. I worked there for seven years, from 1983-1990. During those years, I continued to pray about missionary service and believed that one day the Lord would open the proper door which would allow me to serve as a technical missionary.

Around 1986, I became re-acquainted with the Far East Broadcasting Company through a group called "Intercristo." This is a Christian organization which matches one's interests and education with potential mission agencies – a bit like a Christian referral agency.

In 1988, I visited one of Far East Broadcasting Company's shortwave sites in a place called *Saipan,* a small island in the Western Pacific. I greatly enjoyed this experience and began to pray about the possibility of returning as a full-time missionary.

In 1989, I applied for career missionary status with FEBC and began the process of raising my financial support, which took about a year to complete.

At first, the leadership of FEBC wanted me to serve a one-year term at their San Francisco station and then move on to the Philippines. This was a major test of my faith and commitment since I really wanted to return to Saipan. I made no mention of this to the FEBC leadership but made it a matter for prayer. I distinctly remember praying something like this: "Lord, if you want me to go to San Francisco and the Philippines, I will go. But, Lord, you know that my heart's desire is to return to Saipan. May your will be done." About a week after praying that prayer, I got the word from the FEBC leadership that their plans had changed and that I was heading for Saipan! The words of Psalm 37:4 were certainly true: "Delight yourself also in the Lord, and He shall give you the desires of your heart."

I began my first term of service on Saipan in October of 1990 where I served for the next 18 years. During those years, I greatly enjoyed my role as an engineer for KSAI (our local AM radio station) and KFBS (our international shortwave radio station). Working for the shortwave station was particularly gratifying since millions of people in Russia, China,

Mongolia, Vietnam, and Indonesia were coming to know Christ through the radio ministry.

In 2008, I came back to Alabama in order to take care of my aging parents, Rev. and Mrs. George Creel. During those years, I was on assignment to partner ministry with Galcom International. In that role I designed and built Christian radio stations in various places around the world including Zambia, Albania, Malta, Pohnpei, Paraguay, Belize, and Indonesia.

In 2010, I met Vicki at Brasher Springs Camp Meeting in Gallant, Alabama. Later, at the suggestion of a mutual friend, we began corresponding. We met again in 2013 while Vicki was serving as a volunteer with SIFAT (Servants in Faith and Technology) in Lineville, Alabama. We were married in April 2014.

In 2012, my dad passed away and my mom in 2014. After the death of my parents, Vicki and I were asked to serve on FEBC's International Service Team. Currently we both are serving with FEBC's International Service Team (FEBC IST) providing technical support to our radio stations in Asia.

In my testimony, I have shared a lot about my experiences as a missionary. But remember, we are all called to be missionaries. We are all called to share Christ in appropriate ways with those around us who do not know Him. Each time I leave my home church's parking lot, I see a sign which reads: "You are now entering the mission field." Let that be a challenge to us all. This can involve developing a relationship with someone over a period of time and then sharing Christ at an appropriate moment. This can be done while sharing in another's grief. Or this can be as simple as leaving a gospel tract along with your tip at your favorite restaurant. The point is to find appropriate ways in keeping with your personality, gifts, and talents to share Christ with others.

FEBC Saipan

David - Project in Albania, 2009

David - Project in Malta, 2010

David working with Galcom radios in Canada, 2013

David's parents, Rev. George & Mrs. Jackie Creel, 1997

Chapter 20: CALLED TOGETHER TO THE HARVEST FIELD

Our Story - The man in my dream

"How did the two of you meet?" ask many of our friends. The answer is not straightforward. The Lord used different events in our lives, and with the help of friends, David and I got together. To make a long story short, here is the series of events that brought us together.

In the Fall of 2007, the Lord opened an opportunity for me to come to Alabama with an organization called Servants in Faith and Technology (SIFAT). Together with other Christian and community workers from different countries we had 10 weeks of training in Community Development. From May-December 2008, I served in Ixiamas in the northern part of Bolivia with SIFAT.

In the Spring of 2010, I was invited back to SIFAT to help in the training administrative office for a few months.

One morning in summer, Sarah Corson (one of the founders of SIFAT), invited me to go to Brasher Springs Camp Meeting for a few days. Up to that point, I had not heard of Brasher Springs Camp Meeting. It was a summer camp meeting, founded in 1949, emphasizing holiness for youth and adults. Well, I was surely glad I decided to go. I enjoyed the preaching and the Bible Studies. I also liked the morning prayer time. It was fun to see many young people and children enjoying the camp, too.

On the fourth day, Sarah told me we had to go back to SIFAT the following day. On Monday night, after the evening service, I once again joined the *ice cream social and singing* at the cafeteria. I really enjoyed the time of group singing. Since it was already the fourth day, I had met many people. Even though it was not easy to remember all the names, I remember how everyone was nice and welcoming. On that Monday night, during the time of eating ice cream and singing, Sarah's daughter, Kathy Bryson, introduced me to a gentleman named David Creel. According to Kathy, her husband had known David since the days of their youth group meetings in North Alabama. I found out that David was the missionary speaker during that year's encampment. However, there were many people and activities in the room, so we only spoke for a few minutes. Then, I had to leave the following day to return to SIFAT. I thought that was the end of the story.

In the spring of 2011, I felt led to return to China to serve with a children's home. Around Thanksgiving, I received an email from Kathy with an attachment of a newsletter from David Creel. In the newsletter, I found out that David was serving with a ministry called Far East Broadcasting Company (FEBC). Back in the Philippines, for many years, I had listened to the radio programs of DZAS-AM (FEBC Philippines). For more than twenty years, every time I was back in the Philippines, the Christian teachings, and programs of FEBC had been a constant source of encouragement. I sent a short note to David around Christmas 2012 to let him know how much I appreciated the ministry of FEBC. Little did I know that my short note would start something beautiful. We started corresponding via email and Skype at that time.

In March of 2013, after 14 months of serving in the children's home, I had to leave China again. Just in time, SIFAT invited me once again to come and help with their training event. David and I met again in person and got to know more about each other. Our friendship grew and developed. We became more aware that the love of God had brought us together.

Later, I discovered that David was originally scheduled to be the missionary speaker at Brasher Springs in 2009, but due to illness, he was rescheduled for the 2010 encampment. And that was the first time for me to be at the camp. Looking back, we are both amazed how the Lord works in the details of our lives. We praise the Lord as His word says in Romans 8:28: *"All things work together for good to those who love God and who are called according to His purpose."*

On April 27, 2014, David and I were married at the small outdoor Creel Chapel at Camp Sumatanga near Gallant, Alabama. On a stormy day, on top of a hill, with our families and friends, we had a memorable and momentous wedding day.

I'm very grateful, too, that God answered my long-time prayer to serve Him with a man of God of His choosing. The Lord is truly faithful in fulfilling His words.

In 1998, while serving in China, I was praying one time for marriage. I felt the Lord answered me through this verse in I Samuel 1:17, *"Go in peace and may the God of Israel grant you what you have asked of him."*

One day in May 2000, while on furlough in the Philippines, I woke up in the early dawn hours with a dream. I did not remember a face, but I woke up bewildered, saying, "David!" Then I was led to read Psalm 89:20, *"I have found My servant David; With My holy oil I have anointed him..."*

So, when I met David Creel, I asked the Lord, "Is he the man in my dream?"

Since our wedding, we have been serving together as full-time missionaries with Far East Broadcasting Company. The mission of FEBC is to proclaim the Gospel via media to those who have little or no opportunity to hear about the love of God.

We enjoy serving the Lord together. We are experiencing fun and adventure as we travel together, learn about other cultures, and meet new people. In the past six years, we have traveled together about 3 times a year to Asia, usually for about 3-4 weeks at a time. We have visited our radio stations in Thailand, Indonesia, Philippines, South Korea, Mongolia, and Cambodia. David, together with the engineering team, provides technical support. I help with bookkeeping and other administrative support.

It has been a bit of a challenge for me to adjust from being a *front liner* in the mission field to being in a *behind the scenes* role. However, our hearts and goals are the same: to follow the Great Commission given to us in Matthew 28:19, to go and preach the Gospel to those who have not heard.

Wherever we travel, we try to share the love of Jesus and the Gospel with the people we meet. It is interesting that in some places in Asia, we meet people who have not heard of Jesus. When not traveling, we continue to reach people for Jesus anywhere we go. We also make time to visit supporting churches and speak at mission conferences. In our speaking, we *encourage everyone to participate in missions, to follow Jesus' call to His harvest field, whether through praying, giving, or going.* Through technology (such as the internet), David provides remote technical support to the many FEBC fields. Currently (2021), we live in Alabama and are praying for the Lord's guidance and timing for a move to Asia. We are looking forward to the next chapter as we follow our **Lord Jesus' call to His harvest field.**

Leaf for Life Training at SIFAT

Participants from different countries at SIFAT training

Ken & Sarah Corson with daughter Kathy founders of SIFAT

Wedding April 2014, Camp Sumatanga

Brasher Springs Camp Meeting, 2013

Meeting a listener of FEBC Indonesia, 2017

Working at FEBC Cambodia, 2019

Visiting FEBC Mongolia, 2018

AFTERWORD

There was a big wedding feast soon to take place. The young, beautiful bride was excited and had prepared with her friends.

After many days and months of waiting, the big wedding day came! The bride was wearing the most elegant wedding dress, adorned with her best jewelry. The wedding procession began. She rode in a carriage pulled by three horses. Her friends and family were walking, dancing, and rejoicing in front of the carriage!

In a far-away village, the bridegroom was also getting ready. He was dressed in his best, regal wedding garments and mounted his chariot pulled by seven horses. All his friends and family came riding on horses, rejoicing, and celebrating the coming wedding! As in the old tradition, the groom's wedding party made plans to meet the bride and her wedding party in the village square. It took a few days for the groom to get to her village. Everyone was rejoicing and the air was filled with love and excitement as they all waited! He couldn't wait to see his beautiful bride, and she couldn't wait to see her handsome groom.

On the road, while the groom was sitting in his chariot, talking and laughing with his friends, a man came running from the crowd. He came up to the groom, bowing down, gasping for air. He said, "Stop! Greetings my Prince!"

The groom stopped and faced the man. "What is it? Tell me what is this very important news you bring? Do you not know I am going to my wedding?"

"Yes, your highness!" The servant remained bowed down to the ground in reverence to his master. "I understand it is your wedding day." Then he paused again and took another deep breath and said: "I am very sorry to have to bring you some very important news."

The prince, now with exasperation said, "What is it? Tell me, what is this very important news?"

"I saw your bride, with her friends." Then he paused again, and continued, "While on their way to the wedding place a group of bandits came suddenly from nowhere and took your bride! I am very sorry. They were riding on swift horses, and they vanished into the forest." The prince-groom dismounted from his chariot and tore his clothes and cried, "Oh, my princess bride; oh, my princess bride!"

The bridegroom, his heart broken, cried for many days. His heart yearned for his beautiful bride. From that moment on, with the help of his friends, the prince began the search to rescue his bride.

Yes, this story sounds like a movie plot. However, this is not from a movie that I watched nor from a novel I read. I heard a very similar fictional story from a former instructor during my missions training. The late Dr. Daniel Tappeiner (who was a professor at the Asian Seminary of Christian Ministries) told this story, which I have expanded and illustrated to parallel the story of Jesus and His Bride. The bride represents the people of God waiting to be rescued from the devil who came to steal and to destroy. Jesus is like the groom who is waiting to rescue and save His people. (John 10:10)

The heart of Jesus is to rescue and save His people. His heart yearns and longs for His bride to be delivered from the evil one. This is the heart of missions, the heart of God, to save and deliver people from sin and the evil one. When Dr. Tappeiner told this story in my mission class, the story left a mark on me.

As friends of the bridegroom, we are to be part of the rescue mission. The apostle Peter wrote, "The Lord is ... longsuffering toward us, not willing that any should perish but that all should come to repentance." (2 Peter 3:9)

"After these things I looked, and behold, a great multitude which no one could number, of all nations, tribes, peoples, and tongues, standing before the throne and before the Lamb, clothed with white robes, with palms branches in their hands, and crying out with a loud voice, saying, 'Salvation belongs to our God who sits on the throne, and to the Lamb." (Revelation 7:9)

"Let us be glad and rejoice and give him glory, for the marriage of the Lamb has come, and His wife has made herself ready...Then he said to me, 'Write: Blessed are those who are called to the marriage supper of the Lamb! ...'" (Revelation 19:7,9)

SPECIAL THANKS

I would like to take this opportunity to praise and thank the Lord for the following men and women of God who have inspired me to stay faithful in following Jesus' call to His harvest field:

Dr. Miguel and Mrs. Mireya Alvarez (Church of God World Missions); Ms. Meg Alag (ACM); Ms. Gill Edgar; Ken & Sarah Corson (SIFAT); Ms. Ann Toraya; Dr. Charles & Mrs. Sherry Quinley (Media Light Asia); the Mayfields.

For those who supported me in prayer and finances, thank you very much:

Lighthouse Christian Community; Word for the World Christian Fellowship – Greenhills; Asian Center for Mission; Acts 13 Initiative; Pastor Paul Ignacio; His1040 Inc.; Far East Broadcasting Company (FEBC).

Thank you also to those who have prayed and supported me in the past and those who are currently supporting David and me to follow Jesus's call to His harvest field. May our Lord Jesus bless you all!

ABOUT THE AUTHORS

Vicki Creel grew up in a small town in the Philippines. She received Jesus Christ as her Lord and Savior in 1985 during her senior year in high school. In 1992, while working for a retail company, she received the call of Jesus to serve in missions. In 1997, after training with Asian Center for Mission, she moved to a remote city in China, where she lived for more than 10 years, sharing the love of Jesus. In 2007, Vicki took Community Development Training with Servants in Faith and Technology (SIFAT) in Alabama. In 2008, she served for a few months at SIFAT's children's home in Bolivia. Besides English and her native language Tagalog, Vicki also speaks Mandarin and some Spanish.

David Creel grew up in Alabama and is the son of the late Rev. and Mrs. George Creel. He has served as a missionary engineer with Far East Broadcasting Company (FEBC) since 1990. He worked for 18 years at FEBC's shortwave radio station on the island of Saipan. David also helped build radio stations with Galcom International in Albania, Malta, Paraguay, Belize, Pohnpei, and some remote islands in Indonesia.

In 2010, David and Vicki met in Alabama. In 2014 they were married and now serve together with FEBC. They currently live in Alabama providing technical support for FEBC's radio stations in Asia. They now share adventures in the mission field as they travel and visit FEBC's radio stations in Mongolia, Cambodia, Indonesia, Korea, and the Philippines. Their passion is for more people to know the love of God, especially those who have not heard the Good News of salvation that Jesus offers. They share their inspirational messages in their web blog - thecreels.org.

NOTES

i In the Philippines, during the 1970's, public schools began education at the first grade, not kindergarten.

ii Summer vacation in the Philippines is usually in April and May.

iii In the Philippines educational system, prior to year 2010, students had 6 years of elementary school, 4 years of high school, and then college.

iv One peso was worth approximately a dime (US ten cents) during the mid-1990s in the Philippines.

v Unreached People Group (UPG) - "Unreached groups lack enough followers of Christ and resources to evangelize their own people." - Joshua Project (joshuaproject.net).

vi "The 10/40 Window is the rectangular area of North Africa, the Middle East and Asia approximately between 10 degrees north and 40 degrees north latitude. The 10/40 Window is often called "The Resistant Belt" and includes the majority of the world's Muslims, Hindus, and Buddhists. The original 10/40 Window included only countries with at least 50% of their land mass within 10- and 40-degrees north latitude." *Joshua Project* *h*ttps://joshuaproject.net/resources/articles/10_40_window accessed June 14, 2021.

vii Cultural Revolution, "an upheaval launched by Chinese Communist Party Chairman Mao Zedong during his last decade in power (1966-76) to renew the spirit of the Chinese Revolution." – Kenneth G. Lieberthal

"Cultural Revolution," *Brittanica*, https://www.britannica.com/event/Cultural-Revolution, accessed February 11, 2021.

[viii] Tibetan people group – is part of the 55 officially recognized ethnic groups in China.

[ix] Mao suit - traditional Chinese style clothing made of cotton. ("The name **"Mao suit"** comes from Chinese Communist leader Mao Zedong's fondness for the style, so that the garment became closely associated with him and with Chinese Communism.") *Wikipedia*, https://en.wikipedia.org/wiki/Mao_suit, accessed February 11, 2021.

[x] According to Joshua Project, China has 544 People Groups – "People Groups: China," *Joshua Project* https://joshuaproject.net/countries/CH, accessed February 11, 2021.

[xi] "One-child policy, official program initiated in the late 1970s and early 1980s by the central government of China, the purpose of which was to limit the great majority of family units in the country to one child each. The rationale for implementing the policy was to reduce the growth rate of China's enormous population. It was announced in late 2015 that the program was to end in early 2016."

Pletcher, Kenneth. "One-child policy." *Encyclopedia Britannica*, May 12, 2020, https://www.britannica.com/topic/one-child-policy. Accessed February 11, 2021.

[xii] Kang, C.H. & Nelson, Ethel, The Discovery of Genesis: How the Truths of Genesis Were Found Hidden in the

Chinese Language; St. Louis, Concordia Publishing House, 1979.

[xiii]"Myalgic Encephalomyelitis (ME), commonly referred to as chronic fatigue syndrome, is a serious, debilitating, chronic disease that affects multiple body systems, including the nervous system, the immune system, and the body's production of energy." "'Myalgic Encephalomyelitic - 'Chronic Fatigue Syndrome'", Department of Health, New York State. http://health.ny.gov, May 2018, http://health.ny.gov/diseases/conditions/me-cfs/

[xiv] "The Three Self Church emerged in the last half century, as a Chinese-Led denomination moving apart from the Western denominations. Its name comes from its commitment to wresting control from the Westerners: the three selves are self-support (financial), self-leadership and self-propagation." Grant Paul, *Urbana.org, Intervarsity Urbana Student Mission* Conference, The Three Self Patriotic Movement in China, https://urbana.org/blog/three-self-patriotic-movement-china, October 18, 2011.

www.ingramcontent.com/pod-product-compliance
Lightning Source LLC
Chambersburg PA
CBHW051424290426
44109CB00016B/1420